# VEGAN
# SLOW COOKER

## SASKIA SIDEY

hamlyn

First published in Great Britain in 2021 by Hamlyn,
an imprint of Octopus Publishing Group Ltd
Carmelite House
50 Victoria Embankment
London EC4Y 0DZ
www.octopusbooks.co.uk

An Hachette UK Company
www.hachette.co.uk

Distributed in the US by
Hachette Book Group
1290 Avenue of the Americas
4th and 5th Floors
New York, NY 10104

Distributed in Canada by Canadian Manda Group
664 Annette Street, Toronto, Ontario,
Canada M6S 2C8

ISBN 978-0-60063-695-3

A CIP catalogue record for
this book is available from the
British Library.

Printed and bound in China.

10 9 8 7 6 5 4 3 2 1

Senior Commissioning Editor: Louise McKeever
Senior Editor: Pauline Bache
Copyeditor: Jo Richardson
Senior Designer: Jaz Bahra
Designer: Fiona Gacki
Photographer: William Shaw
Food Stylist: Saskia Sidey
Props Stylist: Jenny Iggleden
Senior Production Manager: Katherine Hockley

# CONTENTS

# INTRODUCTION

*So why use a slow cooker to make your vegan dishes?*

### It's quick and easy

No babysitting your dinner, no constant stirring at the stove – a slow cooker makes light work of big hearty dishes. While they may take longer to cook than traditional recipes using a hob or oven, the time you save on prep is invaluable.

### It's healthy

You can extract the maximum flavour from your ingredients, locking in their nutrients without the need for lots of cooking fats.

### It's cheaper

Not only can you make the most out of inexpensive root vegetables, and use dried herbs instead of fresh, slow cookers use far less electricity to power than other cooking methods, saving you even more money.

### It's portable

You can take your slow cooker with you anywhere – use it on camping trips, take it to a holiday rental or just set it up in the living room when you're catering for large groups and don't have the counter space.

### A note on slow cooker capacity

All the recipes were tested in a 6.5 litre (11½ pint) slow cooker, so adjust quantities and cooking times according to the capacity of your slow cooker if necessary. Take particular care with baking recipes: if using a 3.6 litre (6 pint) slow cooker, instead of baking the batter in a 900 g (2 lb) loaf tin where instructed, line the bottom and sides of the slow cooker pot with nonstick baking paper and add the batter directly; and for the Cherry Bakewell Breakfast Cake (see page 10) and PB & J French Toast Bake (see page 14), halve the ingredient quantities.

# SLOW COOKER TOP TIPS

Follow these simple guidelines to ensure successful slow cooking every time.

## Less is more
If you're adapting one of your favourite recipes to be made in the slow cooker, be sure to reduce the liquid content by at least one-third, if not one-half. Because of the tight-fitting lid and prolonged cooking process, most of the liquid will not evaporate from a slow cooker, so you could end up with a thin, runny sauce. If this does happen, transfer the cooking liquid to a saucepan and simmer briskly, uncovered, on the hob until reduced, or remove 2 tablespoons of the cooking liquid and mix with 1 tablespoon cornflour in a cup until smooth, return to the pan and simmer for a few minutes, stirring, until thickened.

## Layer flavours
Although a lot of the time it can be tempting to skip preliminary stages like sautéeing onions and garlic, toasting spices or marinating vegetables, these steps will add deep flavour to your dishes. You can, of course, just throw all the ingredients into the slow cooker to cook, but you might end up with something a little less tasty.

## Consider temperature
Be mindful of whether your ingredients are fridge-cold before going into the slow cooker – this will affect cooking times. Make sure any stock in the recipe is boiling hot before it's added, or again this will significantly delay the cooking process. If you're in a hurry, you can also preheat your slow cooker while you prep.

## Keep greens fresh
Slow cooking some green vegetables can lead to them looking a bit brown and sludgy. Unless otherwise instructed, always add leafy green vegetables and fresh herbs at the last minute to keep things vibrant.

## Put a lid on it (sometimes)
We always want to peek into our slow cooker to check on progress, but it's important to resist the urge, as opening the lid lets the carefully calibrated temperature of the slow cooker dip and can affect your dish. Each time you open the lid will add about 15 minutes to the cooking time. However, when baking certain dishes or attempting to reduce liquid in a dish, it's often advisable to place a tea towel or kitchen paper underneath the lid to trap the steam, or to position the lid slightly ajar for some of the cooking time to allow steam to escape, as directed in the recipes.

### Make cleaning up a breeze

Where possible, grease your slow cooker pot to avoid any stuck-on food at the end of the cooking process. When baking or cooking a very sticky mixture, line the pot with nonstick baking paper, or stock up on specially designed plastic slow cooker liners that can prevent burnt bottoms and crusty slow cooker pots.

### Be flexible

Slow cooking is not the most intuitive way to cook, and different models of slow cooker run at slightly different temperatures, so you have to keep a degree of flexibility with cooking times and get to know your own cooker. A recipe that says it takes 2 hours to cook could be ready in closer to half that time in some slow cookers.

### Highs and lows

Most slow cookers have two functions: 'high' and 'low'. If you want to cook something for longer than stated, or need it on the table sooner, as a general rule of thumb it takes twice as long to cook something on low than on high. For example, if a recipe states 8 hours on low, you could cook it for 4 hours on high instead.

### Reheating and storing

Don't use your ceramic slow cooker pot to store leftovers, as it's designed to keep the contents warm for extended periods of time and can lead to harmful bacteria breeding. Similarly, do not use your slow cooker to reheat leftovers, as harmful bacteria can reproduce in the time it takes for the pot to heat up.

### Prep like a pro

When preparing your ingredients, think carefully about the size you are cutting your vegetables into. Are you cooking on low for 10 hours? Make the pieces bigger so that they don't turn into mush. Need dinner on the table in an hour? Cut them as small as you can to ensure even cooking in a short space of time. Plan ahead certain recipes that you can prep for in advance – any that call for all ingredients just to be dropped into the slow cooker can be chopped and prepared, frozen in freezer bags, defrosted and then cooked straight away.

### Timing is everything

A lot of slow cookers don't have built-in timers, so make sure you have one nearby for setting the cooking time – I have attached a kitchen timer to the lid of my slow cooker – because it's very easy to lose track of whatever you're cooking and ruin dinner!

### Stay steady and safe

Make sure your slow cooker is on a secure flat surface away from anything flammable or delicate – the outside of the cooker can get very hot, so you need to be careful when handling it.

# VEGAN INGREDIENTS

Certain ingredients can sometimes contain hidden animal products. Always make sure you double check the food label on the packaging before purchasing. There are, of course, vegan alternatives to all these items, but it's important to keep these in mind when shopping.

### Bread
Some bread can contain milk or butter.

### Chocolate
Vegan chocolate should be labelled as such, but look out for 'whey' or 'casein' on dark chocolate labels – don't assume that all 70% cocoa dark chocolate is dairy free.

### Citrus fruit
The wax routinely found on citrus fruits such as lemons, limes and oranges contains shellac or beeswax, which are insect by-products, so buy unwaxed wherever possible.

### Dairy-free cheese
Some dairy-free soya-based cheeses can still contain casein, so make sure you look for the vegan certification.

### Icing sugar
This type of sugar can contain dried egg white, so double check the ingredients list.

### Jam
Some jams contain gelatine as a thickener rather than the traditional (and vegan) pectin.

### Margarine
If using margarine instead of vegan butter, while most margarines are made from vegetable fats, some can be blended with yogurt or contain other animal proteins, so check the label carefully.

### Pre-packaged foods
Even if a product is vegetable based – vegetable soup, for example – it can sometimes contain milk powders or egg as a thickener. Double check condiments such as pesto, barbecue sauce and bottled salad dressings.

### Vinegar
Vinegar can contain animal proteins. Vegetarian vinegars are available but always check the label. Alternatively, all distilled vinegars and malt vinegars are vegetarian, and acidic flavours such as lemon juice can also be used in their place.

### Wine, cider & beer
These items can contain animal proteins, used in the fermentation, clarifiying and fining processes, so always double check the label.

### Worcestershire sauce
Non-vegan Worcestershire sauce traditionally contains anchovies.

# BREAKFASTS

*This is the closest you can get to eating dessert for breakfast without feeling guilty. Swap the dried cherries for other dried fruit of your choice, such as raisins, sultanas, dried cranberries or roughly chopped dried apricots, or try fresh cherries or raspberries or blackberries when in season.*

**MAKES 6–8 SLICES • PREPARATION TIME 15 MINUTES • COOKING TIME 1–1½ HOURS**

# CHERRY BAKEWELL BREAKFAST CAKE

70 ml (2½ fl oz) melted coconut, vegetable or sunflower oil

200 ml (7 fl oz) unsweetened almond milk

finely grated zest and juice of 1 unwaxed lemon

120 ml (4 fl oz) maple syrup

1 teaspoon vanilla bean paste

½ teaspoon salt

150 g (5 oz) ground almonds

150 g (5 oz) self-raising flour

½ teaspoon bicarbonate of soda

½ teaspoon baking powder

150 g (5 oz) dried cherries

20 g (¾ oz) flaked almonds

Line the bottom of the slow cooker pot with nonstick baking paper so that it comes at least 2 cm (¾ inch) up the sides.

Whisk together the oil, almond milk, lemon zest and juice, maple syrup, vanilla bean paste, salt and ground almonds in a large bowl until well combined. Sift in the flour, bicarbonate of soda and baking powder and fold in gently. Add in three-quarters of the dried cherries and fold in gently.

Pour the batter into the slow cooker and spread it out evenly. Sprinkle the flaked almonds and remaining cherries on top.

Place a tea towel or kitchen paper underneath the slow cooker lid, cover the cooker and bake on high for 1–1½ hours until springy but firm to the touch and very lightly golden.

Remove the pot from the slow cooker and leave the cake to cool in the pot slightly. Then use the lining paper to lift the cake out of the pot and leave to cool on a wire rack. Serve warm, with some dairy-free yogurt and a dollop of cherry jam if you like, or leave to cool completely. Store in an airtight container for up to 4 days.

*Blueberries are the obvious choice for fruity muffins, particularly as they freeze so well and are easy to stash in the freezer. But feel free to use other fresh berries, or even vegan dark chocolate chips. It's essential to use silicone muffin cases (or mini pudding tins, though you may only be able to fit 5 in your slow cooker), as paper muffin cases aren't sturdy enough to withstand the slow cooking process.*

**MAKES 6–8 SMALL OR 5–6 LARGE MUFFINS • PREPARATION TIME 15 MINUTES, PLUS STANDING • COOKING TIME 1½ HOURS**

# BLUEBERRY MUFFINS

vegan butter, for greasing (optional)

125 ml (4 fl oz) dairy-free milk, such as soya or almond milk

½ teaspoon apple cider vinegar

2 tablespoons sunflower or vegetable oil

½ teaspoon vanilla bean paste

175 g (6 oz) plain flour

75 g (3 oz) caster sugar

1½ teaspoons baking powder

1 teaspoon bicarbonate of soda

½ teaspoon salt

finely grated zest of 1 unwaxed lemon

125 g (4 oz) fresh or frozen blueberries

Put 8 silicone fairy cake cases or 6 silicone muffin cases (or 5 or 6 greased mini pudding tins, depending on how many fit) into the slow cooker pot.

Mix together the dairy-free milk and vinegar in a bowl and leave to curdle for about 10 minutes.

Add the oil and vanilla bean paste and whisk together until well combined.

Mix together all the remaining ingredients, except the blueberries, in a large separate bowl. Then gradually fold in the dairy-free milk mixture and blueberries until well combined.

Add approximately 2 tablespoons of batter to each fairy cake case or muffin case or pudding tin. Place a tea towel or kitchen paper underneath the slow cooker lid, cover the cooker and cook on high for 1½ hours until the muffins are domed and firm to the touch.

Remove from the slow cooker and serve warm, or leave to cool completely on a wire rack. Store in an airtight container for up to 5 days.

*Take the base formula for this French toast bake and experiment with different flavour combinations – swap the peanut butter and jam for melted vegan chocolate, or go down the savoury route with some vegan cheese.*

**SERVES 4 • PREPARATION TIME 15 MINUTES, PLUS STANDING
COOKING TIME 1–1½ HOURS**

# PB & J FRENCH TOAST BAKE

½ tablespoon sunflower or
  vegetable oil, for greasing
2 tablespoons ground flaxseed
  (linseed)
50 g (2 oz) vegan butter, melted
200 ml (7 fl oz) unsweetened
  almond milk
3 tablespoons smooth peanut
  butter
½ teaspoon ground cinnamon
¼ teaspoon ground nutmeg
½ teaspoon baking powder
250 g (8 oz) stale sourdough,
  cut into large cubes

TO SERVE
icing sugar
3 tablespoons jam of your choice
roasted, unsalted peanuts,
  roughly chopped

Grease the slow cooker pot with the oil.

Put the ground flaxseed, melted vegan butter, almond milk, peanut butter and spices into the slow cooker, use a whisk to break up the peanut butter and whisk until the mixture is emulsifed. Leave to stand for 5–10 minutes until slightly thickened.

Stir in the baking powder, add the bread cubes and toss until well coated in the mixture.

Place a tea towel or kitchen paper underneath the slow cooker lid, cover the cooker and cook on high for 1–1½ hours until springy but firm to the touch and the remaining liquid is thickened, golden and bubbly.

Serve immediately, dusted with icing sugar, drizzled with jam and scattered with chopped roasted peanuts.

*Using a loaf tin inside your slow cooker is a great hack to create a traditional, sliceable loaf. Alternatively, you can simply grease and line the bottom of the slow cooker pot with nonstick baking paper and pour in the batter, reduce the cooking time by about 30 minutes and cut the cooked 'loaf' into bars. Try varying the ingredients, using roughly chopped dried apricots or other dried fruit instead of the raisins or sultanas, or vegan dark chocolate chips in place of the dried fruit, or swap the mixed nuts for pecans.*

**MAKES ONE 900 G (2 LB) LOAF • PREPARATION TIME 15 MINUTES
COOKING TIME 1½–2 HOURS**

# SEEDY BANANA BREAKFAST LOAF

nonstick cooking spray or vegan
   butter, for greasing
3 large or 4 small very ripe
   bananas
60 g (2¼ oz) soya or oat yogurt
50 ml (2 fl oz) sunflower or
   vegetable oil
75 g (3 oz) light brown soft sugar
200 g (7 oz) plain flour
10 g (⅓ oz) baking powder
1 teaspoon ground mixed spice
1 teaspoon ground cinnamon
75 g (3 oz) mixed nuts, roughly
   chopped
75 g (3 oz) raisins or sultanas
25 g (1 oz) mixed seeds, such as
   flaxseed (linseed), pumpkin
   and sunflower

Line the bottom and sides of a silicone or metal 900 g (2 lb) loaf tin with nonstick baking paper and grease with nonstick cooking spray or vegan butter. Ensure that the tin fits snugly inside the slow cooker pot, using some scrunched-up balls of foil to raise the tin slightly off the bottom, or to secure it if it doesn't quite reach the cooker bottom.

Mash the bananas in a large bowl, then mix in the yogurt, oil and sugar.

Sift the flour, baking powder and spices into the bowl, then fold in gently to combine until almost no dry patches remain. Gently fold in the nuts, dried fruit and seeds.

Pour the batter into the prepared loaf tin, cover with the lid and cook on high for 2 hours until the top of the loaf looks dry and a skewer inserted into the centre comes out clean, but check for doneness after 1½ hours and thereafter at frequent intervals until cooked.

Remove from the slow cooker and leave to cool in the tin for 10 minutes. Then use the lining paper to lift the loaf out of the tin and leave to cool on a wire rack.

Slice and serve still warm, leave to cool completely or toast and spread with vegan butter and jam. Store in an airtight container for up to 4 days.

*I've used steel cut oats here, which are also known as pinhead oats or coarse oatmeal. They take longer to cook than rolled oats in the traditional way but, as you are using a slow-cooking method anyway, you can take advantage of their hearty texture and nutty flavour without any extra effort. If you only have rolled oats, just reduce the cooking time by 30 minutes.*

**SERVES 2–3 • PREPARATION TIME 10 MINUTES, PLUS INFUSING**
**COOKING TIME 4–5 HOURS**

# CHAI & BANANA OATS

nonstick cooking spray, for greasing (optional)
1 chai tea bag
300 ml (½ pint) boiling water
400 ml (14 fl oz) almond, soya or light coconut milk
175 g (6 oz) steel cut oats (pinhead oats or coarse oatmeal)
1 ripe banana, mashed
pinch of salt

Grease the slow cooker pot liberally with nonstick cooking spray or line the bottom and sides with nonstick baking paper. Alternatively, place a smaller nonstick bowl inside the slow cooker pot and add 2–3 cm (¾–1¼ inches) of water to the slow cooker pot, to act as a bain-marie (water bath).

Steep the tea bag in the measured boiling water for 10 minutes until you have a dark and fragrant infusion, then remove the tea bag.

Put the tea infusion into the slow cooker and add the remaining ingredients. Cover with the lid and cook on low for 4–5 hours; the longer cooking time results in a thicker consistency. If your slow cooker has the function to switch over automatically to 'keep warm' once the cooking time is up, leave to cook overnight. Alternatively, set a separate timer to make sure the oats don't overcook and burn.

Serve warm, topped with sliced banana, blueberries and toasted nuts (almonds or walnuts work well) if you like.

*Start off your day on the bright side with this sunny yellow porridge. The turmeric is optional, as are the toppings, which can also be varied – try sliced banana or blueberries and sesame seeds, or a pinch of ground cinnamon with stewed fruit.*

**SERVES 2–3 • PREPARATION TIME 5 MINUTES • COOKING TIME 4–6 HOURS**

# OVERNIGHT TURMERIC PORRIDGE

100 g (3½ oz) rolled oats
700 ml (1¼ pints) almond, soya
   or light coconut milk
2 teaspoons ground turmeric
   (optional)
2 tablespoons demerara sugar
1 teaspoon vanilla bean paste
pinch of salt

TO SERVE
slices of mango
pomegranate seeds
toasted coconut flakes

Put all the ingredients into the slow cooker, cover with the lid and cook on low for 4–6 hours. If your slow cooker has the function to switch over automatically to 'keep warm' once the cooking time is up, leave to cook overnight. Alternatively, set a separate timer to make sure the porridge doesn't overcook and burn.

Give the porridge a good stir before serving, as it will probably have a slight crust on top. Loosen with a dash of water or extra dairy-free milk if it seems dry.

Serve warm, topped with sliced mango, pomegranate seeds and toasted coconut flakes, and drizzled with maple syrup if you like.

*It always amazes me that you are able to make something so crunchy in the slow cooker, and this is a perfect way to use up the odds and ends of packets of nuts and dried fruit that always seem to lurk in the back of the storecupboard. Keep the quantities of oats, fat and maple syrup consistent, and play around with everything else!*

**MAKES ONE 1 LITRE (1¾ PINT) JAR  •  PREPARATION TIME 10 MINUTES, PLUS COOLING COOKING TIME 2–2½ HOURS**

# SALTED MAPLE GRANOLA

100 g (3½ oz) coconut oil or vegan butter, melted

400 g (13 oz) rolled oats

50 ml (2 fl oz) maple syrup

100 g (3½ oz) unsalted nuts, such as almonds, pecans or walnuts, or a mixture, kept whole or roughly chopped

25 g (1 oz) mixed seeds, such as flaxseed (linseed), pumpkin and sunflower

1 tablespoon sea salt flakes

½ teaspoon vanilla bean paste

½ teaspoon ground cinnamon

100 g (3½ oz) dried fruit, such as raisins, dried cherries, dried cranberries or roughly chopped dried apricots

Grease the slow cooker pot with 1 teaspoon of the coconut oil or vegan butter.

Mix together all the remaining ingredients, except the dried fruit, in a large bowl until well combined.

Transfer the granola mixture to the slow cooker and cover with the lid but position it slightly ajar. Cook on high for 2–2½ hours until the mixture is golden and crunchy. Stir 2–3 times during the cooking time to make sure the granola isn't catching on the bottom, but don't be too vigorous so that you keep big clusters of the mixture.

Stir the dried fruit through the granola. Transfer to a tray, spread out and leave to cool completely and crisp up further.

Store in a clean airtight jar for up to 2 weeks.

*This is a wonderful brunch dish to serve with little effort. Accompany it with some warm flatbreads, and top with whatever you fancy – try avocado and vegan yogurt.*

**SERVES 4 • PREPARATION TIME 15 MINUTES, PLUS PRESSING
COOKING TIME 2 HOURS**

# TOFU SHAKSHUKA

2 tablespoons extra virgin
   olive oil
1 onion, finely chopped
400 g (13 oz) can chopped
   tomatoes
2–3 roasted red peppers from
   a jar, drained and chopped
2 garlic cloves, thinly sliced
1 teaspoon ground cumin
1 teaspoon cayenne pepper
1 teaspoon sweet paprika
350 g (11½ oz) firm tofu
salt and pepper

TO SERVE
1 avocado, sliced
small handful of coriander and
   flat leaf parsley, chopped
chilli flakes
flatbreads, warmed

Put 1 tablespoon of the oil, the onion, tomatoes, red peppers, garlic and spices into the slow cooker and toss until well combined. Season to taste with salt and pepper. Cover with the lid and cook on high for 2 hours until the mixture is slightly reduced. Check and adjust the seasoning.

Meanwhile, drain the tofu well, sit on a sheet of kitchen paper and top with a second piece of kitchen paper. Place a heavy bowl or chopping board on top and leave to press for 20–30 minutes, replacing the sheets of kitchen paper if or when they become oversaturated in liquid.

Preheat the oven to 200°C (400°F), Gas Mark 6. Cut the tofu into 2.5 cm (1 inch) cubes, toss with the remaining tablespoon of oil and season with salt and pepper. Spread out on a baking tray and roast in the oven for 25–30 minutes until golden and crispy.

Serve the shakshuka topped with the roasted tofu and sliced avocado, sprinkled with the chopped herbs and a few chilli flakes, with the warm flatbreads on the side.

*Serve as part of a fry-up with grilled tomatoes, garlic mushrooms, baked beans and toast. Alternatively, you can add chopped cherry tomatoes, peppers, spring onions and/or other vegetables to the slow cooker along with the tofu and other ingredients for a complete breakfast in itself.*

**SERVES 2–3 • PREPARATION TIME 10 MINUTES • COOKING TIME 1½ HOURS**

# SCRAMBLED TOFU

3 tablespoons light olive oil
400 g (13 oz) firm tofu, drained, patted dry and crumbled, leaving some big chunks
2 tablespoons dairy-free milk
1 garlic clove, finely chopped or crushed
½ teaspoon ground turmeric
lemon juice, to taste
salt and pepper

Put all the ingredients, except the lemon juice, into the slow cooker and toss until well combined. Season to taste with salt and pepper. Cover with the lid and cook on high for 1½ hours, stirring once halfway through cooking, until the tofu has set, turned pale yellow in colour and started to brown and caramelize in places.

Season to taste with lemon juice, check and adjust the salt and pepper seasoning and serve immediately.

*These slow-cooked baked beans have bags more flavour than the canned ones. I've used cannellini beans here, but you can try pinto, butter beans or haricot, or a mixture. You can also enjoy the beans with jacket potatoes for lunch.*

**SERVES 8 • PREPARATION TIME 10 MINUTES, PLUS SOAKING COOKING TIME 8 HOURS**

# FANCY BAKED BEANS

750 g (1½ lb) dried cannellini beans

400 g (13 oz) can chopped tomatoes

500 ml (17 fl oz) hot vegan bouillon stock

2 shallots, finely chopped

1 tablespoon apple cider vinegar, or more to taste

1 teaspoon vegan Worcestershire sauce

1 teaspoon smoked paprika

2 tablespoons tomato purée

1 teaspoon Marmite

2 thyme sprigs

2 bay leaves

salt and pepper

Soak the dried beans in plenty of fresh cold water for at least 8 hours or overnight. Drain and rinse well.

Put the soaked beans, with all the remaining ingredients, into the slow cooker and season well with salt and pepper. Cover with the lid and cook on low for 8 hours until the beans are tender and the sauce has thickened and reduced.

Check the seasoning and add a dash more vinegar if needed. Serve immediately, on toast if you like.

*The slow cooker is the perfect vessel for making incredibly convincing unctuous 'refried' beans without the frying. Besides serving them in breakfast wraps with all the toppings, you can simply enjoy them straight from the bowl for lunch. These beans freeze really well once cooked, so they are perfect for batch cooking. Try using black beans or kidney beans instead of pinto beans if you can't find them.*

**SERVES 8 • PREPARATION TIME 15 MINUTES • COOKING TIME 8 HOURS**

# 'REFRIED' BEAN WRAPS

2 tablespoons olive oil

1 onion, finely chopped

3 garlic cloves, finely chopped or crushed

450 g (14½ oz) dried pinto beans

1.4 litres (2½ pints) hot vegetable stock

2 teaspoons ground cumin

1 teaspoon chilli powder

½ teaspoon dried oregano

juice of 1 lime

salt and pepper

TO SERVE

tortilla wraps

mashed avocado

tomato salsa

lime wedges

coriander sprigs

Put all the main ingredients, except the lime juice, with 2 teaspoons salt into the slow cooker, cover with the lid and cook on low for 8 hours until the beans are tender.

Reserve a mugful of the cooking liquid, then drain the beans and use a potato masher to mash the mixture to a chunky purée or use an immersion blender to blend until smooth. Season with the lime juice and additional salt and pepper to taste. Add a little of the reserved cooking liquid if you prefer a looser consistency (the bean mixture will thicken as it cools).

Serve warm on tortilla wraps, with the mashed avocado, tomato salsa, lime wedges and coriander sprigs served alongside, for everyone to help themselves to.

# MAINS: 3 HOURS OR LESS

*This spicy soup can have quite a kick, depending on the brand of kimchi you choose.*

**SERVES 4 • PREPARATION TIME 15 MINUTES • COOKING TIME 1 HOUR 40 MINUTES**

# KIMCHI NOODLE SOUP

4 spring onions, finely sliced, plus extra to serve

4 garlic cloves, finely chopped

20 g (¾ oz) fresh root ginger, peeled and cut into fine matchsticks

50 g (2 oz) dried shiitake mushrooms

4 tablespoons light soy sauce, or more to taste

1.5 litres (2½ pints) boiling water

100 g (3½ oz) kimchi, drained

200 g (7 oz) dried ramen noodles or buckwheat soba noodles

2 tablespoons lime juice

Put the spring onions, garlic, ginger, dried mushrooms, soy sauce and measured boiling water into the slow cooker, cover with the lid and cook on high for 1½ hours.

Stir in the kimchi and noodles, replace the lid and cook, still on high, for a further 5–10 minutes until the noodles are tender. Season the soup with the lime juice and more soy sauce if needed.

Serve immediately, topped with extra finely sliced spring onions.

*If you can't find fresh corn, it's fine to use frozen sweetcorn kernels instead – about 400 g (13 oz). You can get creative with the toppings/garnishes here instead of using charred corn and chilli – sprinkle with finely chopped coriander or parsley, or scatter croutons on top too.*

**SERVES 4 • PREPARATION TIME 25 MINUTES • COOKING TIME 1–1½ HOURS**

# CORN CHOWDER

2 tablespoons olive oil

1 large onion, finely sliced, or 1 leek, trimmed, cleaned and finely sliced

2 garlic cloves, finely sliced

2 large floury potatoes, peeled and cut into 1 cm (½ inch) cubes

500 ml (17 fl oz) hot vegan bouillon stock

2 thyme sprigs, leaves picked

3 corn on the cob, kernels sliced from the cob, cobs reserved and a large handful of kernels reserved to garnish

juice of 1 unwaxed lemon, zest reserved to garnish

salt and pepper

TO GARNISH

2 red chillies, finely chopped

handful of chives, finely chopped

Heat the oil in a frying pan over a medium heat, add the onion or leek and sauté for about 10 minutes until softened. Add the garlic and cook for a further minute.

Transfer the onion or leek and garlic to the slow cooker and add the potatoes, hot stock, thyme leaves and corn kernels, along with the cobs for extra corn flavour. Cover with the lid and cook on high for 1–1½ hours until the potatoes are easily pierced with a fork. Season with the lemon juice and salt and pepper to taste.

Remove the cobs and serve immediately, sprinkled with the reserved corn kernels, charred in a pan, the reserved lemon zest and the finely chopped chilli and chives.

*There are endless variations of this classic warming Italian soup to try – change it up with rice or peeled potatoes cut into small cubes in place of the pasta, or any type of canned beans you have sitting around. And don't feel restricted by the vegetables in the ingredients list – the purpose of this dish is to make best use of what you have on hand.*

**SERVES 4–6 • PREPARATION TIME 25 MINUTES • COOKING TIME 1 HOUR 50 MINUTES**

# MINESTRONE

2 tablespoons extra virgin olive oil

1 onion, finely chopped

1 carrot, finely chopped

1 celery stick, finely chopped

1 garlic clove, crushed

2 teaspoons tomato purée

500 ml (17 fl oz) hot vegan bouillon stock

400 g (13 oz) can cherry tomatoes

400 g (13 oz) can cannellini or borlotti beans, drained and rinsed

1 oregano or thyme sprig

100 g (3½ oz) dried ditalini or other small pasta

100 g (3½ oz) cavolo nero or Savoy cabbage, shredded

grated Parmesan-style vegan cheese, to serve (optional)

Heat the oil in a large frying pan over a medium-low heat, add the onion, carrot and celery and sauté for about 10 minutes until softened and beginning to colour. Add the garlic and cook for a further minute.

Transfer the vegetable mixture to the slow cooker and add the tomato purée, hot stock, tomatoes and herb sprig. Cover with the lid and cook on high for 1½ hours.

Stir in the pasta and shredded greens, replace the lid and cook, still on high, for a further 20 minutes.

Serve immediately, sprinkled with grated Parmesan-style vegan cheese if you like.

*This wonderfully rustic stew is very food-waste friendly, putting any stale bread and spare cooked vegetables you have on hand to good use. If you want to use up some dried beans, first soak 200 g (7 oz) of them in plenty of fresh cold water for at least 8 hours or overnight. Then drain and rinse well before adding in place of the whole canned beans, using 750 ml (1¼ pints) stock and adding 1 hour to the cooking time.*

**SERVES 4 • PREPARATION TIME 25 MINUTES • COOKING TIME 2½ HOURS**

# TUSCAN RIBOLLITA

3 tablespoons extra virgin olive oil

1 onion, finely chopped

2 carrots, finely chopped

1 celery stick, finely chopped

½ teaspoon fennel seeds

½ teaspoon chilli flakes

2 garlic cloves, grated

400 g (13 oz) can chopped tomatoes

few sprigs each of thyme, flat leaf parsley and oregano

250 ml (8 fl oz) hot vegan bouillon stock

400 g (13 oz) can cannellini beans, drained and rinsed

200 g (7 oz) cavolo nero, thickly shredded

200 g (7 oz) stale bread, torn into pieces

salt and pepper

grated Parmesan-style vegan cheese, to serve

Heat the oil in a large frying pan over a medium-low heat, add the onion, carrots and celery and sauté for about 10 minutes until softened and beginning to colour. Add the fennel seeds, chilli flakes and garlic and cook for a further 2 minutes.

Transfer the vegetable mixture to the slow cooker and add the tomatoes and herb sprigs. If you prefer a thicker soup, blend 50 ml (2 fl oz) of the stock with one-quarter of the beans in a food processor until puréed, or mash together with a fork in a bowl, before adding them to the slow cooker with the rest of the stock and beans. For a thinner soup, just add the hot stock and beans to the slow cooker as they are. Season well with salt and pepper, cover with the lid and cook on high for 2 hours.

Stir in the cavolo nero and bread, replace the lid and cook, still on high, for a further 30 minutes until the soup is substantially thickened.

Check and adjust the seasoning, then serve immediately, sprinkled with grated Parmesan-style vegan cheese.

## FOR THE RISOTTO

3 tablespoons olive oil

2 banana shallots, finely chopped

½ large or 1 small leek, trimmed, cleaned and finely chopped

pinch of salt

300 g (10 oz) Arborio rice

200 ml (7 fl oz) white wine or vermouth

900 ml (1½ pints) hot vegan bouillon stock

2 teaspoons sea salt flakes

200 g (7 oz) frozen peas

## FOR THE WILD GARLIC & PEA PURÉE

100 g (3½ oz) frozen peas, blanched in boiling water for 2 minutes, drained and rinsed under cold water

large handful of flat leaf parsley, plus extra, roughly chopped, to garnish

large handful of wild garlic leaves

finely grated zest and juice of 1 unwaxed lemon, plus extra zest to garnish

4 tablespoons extra virgin olive oil

salt and pepper

grated Parmesan-style vegan cheese, to serve

*This hands-off risotto is wonderfully fresh and vibrant looking and tasting, and can be on the table in less than 2 hours. If wild garlic isn't in season, make the purée with a garlic clove and add a little extra parsley to achieve the vivid green colour.*

**SERVES 4–6 • PREPARATION TIME 35 MINUTES COOKING TIME 1½–1¾ HOURS**

# WILD GARLIC & PEA RISOTTO

Heat the oil for the risotto in a saucepan over a medium heat. Add the shallots and leek with the pinch of salt and sauté for 5 minutes until softened and beginning to colour. Add the rice and toss to coat, then turn the heat up to high and cook, stirring regularly, for 2 minutes until lightly toasted.

Add the white wine or vermouth and allow it to bubble up and reduce until there is no liquid left visible in the pan. Transfer to the slow cooker and add the hot stock and sea salt. Cover with the lid and cook on high for 1¾ hours, stirring once halfway through cooking, until the rice has absorbed most but not all of the liquid and is cooked but still firm to the bite. However, check for doneness after 1½ hours and thereafter at frequent intervals until ready. If it seems too dry, add a splash of water.

Once the risotto is cooked, turn off the slow cooker, add the peas and re-cover, while you make the wild garlic and pea purée. Blitz together all the purée ingredients in a food processor until smooth, adding 1–2 tablespoons of water if necessary. Check and adjust the seasoning.

Stir the purée through the risotto and serve immediately, scattered with grated Parmesan-style vegan cheese and garnished with chopped parsley and lemon zest.

## FOR THE SAUCE

1 red onion, finely chopped

2 garlic cloves, finely chopped

400 g (13 oz) can chopped
   tomatoes

1 tablespoon tomato purée

150 ml (¼ pint) hot vegan
   bouillon stock

1 tablespoon pomegranate
   molasses

1 tablespoon ras-el-hanout

1 tablespoon ground cumin

salt and pepper

## FOR THE MEATBALLS

1 shallot, quartered

1 garlic clove, peeled

15 g (½ oz) fresh root ginger,
   peeled

1 red chilli

large handful of coriander, plus
   extra, chopped, to garnish

1 preserved lemon

400 g (13 oz) meat-free mince

1 slice of stale white bread, torn
   into pieces

½ tablespoon ground cumin

½ tablespoon ground coriander

1 teaspoon ground cinnamon

1 tablespoon Dijon mustard

1 tablespoon tomato purée

2 teaspoons pomegranate
   molasses

1 tablespoon olive oil (optional)

couscous tossed with fruit and
   nuts, to serve (optional)

*Although the ingredients list may look on the long side, it results in wonderfully aromatic vegan meatballs, and you should find many of these items lurking in your storecupboard.*

**SERVES 4 • PREPARATION TIME 30 MINUTES
COOKING TIME 2–2½ HOURS**

# MOROCCAN MEATLESS MEATBALLS

Put all the sauce ingredients into the slow cooker, cover with the lid and cook on high for 1 hour.

Meanwhile, put the shallot, garlic, ginger, chilli and coriander, stalks and all, in a food processor. Halve the preserved lemon, scrape out the flesh with a teaspoon and discard it, finely chop the rind and add to the food processor. Blitz until you have a slightly chunky paste. Add the remaining ingredients, except the oil, season well with salt and pepper and pulse to combine – to make sure the mixture is fully combined, squeeze it together with your hands.

Preheat the oven to 200°C (400°F), Gas Mark 6. Divide the meatball mixture into even pieces, roll each into a small golf ball-sized ball and place on a baking tray lined with nonstick baking paper. Toss the meatballs in the oil to coat and roast in the oven for 15–20 minutes until browned and caramelized. Alternatively, you can skip this step and simply poach the meatballs in the sauce.

Stir the roasted or unroasted meatballs gently into the sauce, replace the lid and cook, still on high, for a further 1–1½ hours until the sauce has reduced and thickened and the meatballs are cooked through.

Serve immediately, being careful when handling the meatballs as they will be quite delicate, sprinkled with the freshly chopped coriander, along with couscous tossed with dried cranberries or raisins and pine nuts or flaked almonds, if you like.

*This is traditionally cooked in a large ceramic dish in the oven so that it becomes deliciously caramelized, but here a similarly rich and unctuous effect is achieved using the slow cooker.*

**SERVES 4 • PREPARATION TIME 15 MINUTES • COOKING TIME 1½ HOURS**

# GREEK TOMATOES & CHICKPEAS

3 tablespoons extra virgin
  olive oil
1 tablespoon finely chopped
  oregano
1 red onion, finely sliced
400 g (13 oz) can chopped
  tomatoes
400 g (13 oz) can chickpeas,
  drained and rinsed
2 garlic cloves, finely chopped
  or crushed
1 carrot, finely chopped

TO SERVE
small handful of flat leaf parsley,
  finely chopped
small handful of dill, finely
  chopped
crusty bread

Put all the ingredients into the slow cooker, cover with the lid and cook on high for 1½ hours until sticky, reduced and sweet.

Serve immediately, sprinkled with the freshly chopped herbs, along with some crusty bread to mop up the juices.

*The crumbled porcini mushrooms add a deep meatiness to this stroganoff. You can use any variety of mushroom you can find, but portobello or flat mushrooms hold their texture well in the slow cooker. If you can't source any sweet smoked paprika, use ½ tablespoon each of regular sweet paprika and smoked paprika instead.*

**SERVES 2 • PREPARATION TIME 20 MINUTES • COOKING TIME 1½ HOURS**

# PORCINI MUSHROOM STROGANOFF

2 tablespoons vegetable oil

6 large portobello or flat mushrooms, sliced

1 large onion, thinly sliced

2 garlic cloves, thinly sliced

1 tablespoon sweet smoked paprika

1 tablespoon tomato purée

1 tablespoon Dijon mustard

20 g (¾ oz) dried porcini mushrooms, crumbled

150 ml (¼ pint) hot vegan bouillon stock

150 ml (¼ pint) dairy-free soured cream

1 teaspoon apple cider vinegar, or more to taste

salt and pepper

TO SERVE

rice or pasta

small handful of flat leaf parsley, chopped

Heat the oil in a large frying pan over a high heat, add the mushrooms and sauté for about 3 minutes on each side until golden brown. Transfer to the slow cooker.

Add the onion to the frying pan and sauté for 5 minutes until beginning to soften and colour, adding the garlic for the last minute of cooking time.

Transfer the onion and garlic mixture to the slow cooker and add all the remaining ingredients, seasoning well with salt and pepper. Cover with the lid and cook on high for 1½ hours until the sauce has thickened and looks creamy.

Check and adjust the seasoning, adding a dash more vinegar if needed, and serve immediately over rice or pasta, sprinkled with the chopped parsley.

*The sweet potatoes blend really well to make a lovely smooth and creamy 'cheese' sauce. It's best to use an immersion blender (or a high-speed blender) to make sure the texture isn't grainy, but if your food processor isn't quite up to the task, you can pass the blended mixture through a sieve. If you can't get your hands on sweet potatoes, butternut squash also works well, though it will take an additional 30–45 minutes to cook.*

**SERVES 4–6 • PREPARATION TIME 20 MINUTES**
**COOKING TIME 2 HOURS 10 MINUTES–2 HOURS 40 MINUTES**

# SWEET POTATO MAC & CHEESE

3 large sweet potatoes (about 500 g/1 lb), peeled and cut into 3–4 cm (1¼–1½ inch) chunks

1 shallot, sliced

2 garlic cloves, sliced

100 g (3½ oz) cashew nuts

5 tablespoons nutritional yeast

1 tablespoon Dijon mustard

300 ml (½ pint) unsweetened almond milk

300 ml (½ pint) hot vegan bouillon stock

¼ teaspoon freshly grated nutmeg

350 g (11½ oz) dried macaroni

1½ tablespoons apple cider vinegar

2 tablespoons vegetable or sunflower oil

100g (3½ oz) panko breadcrumbs

3 sprigs of thyme, leaves picked

salt and pepper

Put the sweet potatoes, shallot, garlic, cashews, nutritional yeast, mustard, almond milk, hot stock, nutmeg and a good grinding of pepper into the slow cooker. Cover with the lid and cook on high for 2–2½ hours until the sweet potato is easily pierced with a fork.

Meanwhile, cook the macaroni in a large saucepan of salted boiling water according to the packet instructions until firm to the bite. Drain, rinse under cold running water until cool and leave to drain.

Use an immersion blender to blend the sweet potato mixture until smooth and creamy, then season to taste with salt and the vinegar. Stir in the cooked macaroni, replace the lid and cook, still on high, for a further 10 minutes until the pasta is warmed through.

To make the breadcrumb topping, heat the oil in a wide-based pan over a medium heat. Add the breadcrumbs and cook, stirring frequently until golden brown.

When the pasta is warmed through, serve immediately, garnished with the toasted breadcrumbs and thyme leaves, with a lightly dressed leafy salad on the side, if you like.

*The ultimate speedy slow-cooker dish, this briny stew is given a bright, zesty boost with lemon and parsley. It's perfect on its own with some crusty bread, or as a side dish in a big spread.*

**SERVES 2 • PREPARATION TIME 25 MINUTES • COOKING TIME 1 HOUR 10 MINUTES**

# BUTTER BEANS WITH FENNEL, CAPERS & OLIVES

3 tablespoons olive oil
2 shallots, finely sliced
1 large fennel bulb, finely sliced
2 garlic cloves, finely sliced
400 g (13 oz) can butter beans, drained and rinsed
350 ml (12 fl oz) hot vegan bouillon stock
100 g (3½ oz) pitted Spanish Gordal olives, halved
100 g (3½ oz) capers in brine, drained
finely grated zest and juice of 1 unwaxed lemon
salt and pepper

very large handful of flat leaf parsley, roughly chopped, to serve

Heat the oil in a frying pan over a medium-low heat, add the shallots and fennel and sauté for about 10 minutes until beginning to soften and colour. Add the garlic and sauté for a further 1–2 minutes.

Transfer the shallot mixture to the slow cooker and add the butter beans and hot stock. Cover with the lid and cook on high for 1 hour.

Stir in the olives and capers, replace the lid and cook, still on high, for a further 5–10 minutes until warmed through.

Add the lemon zest and juice, season to taste with salt and pepper and serve immediately, sprinkled with the parsley.

*This pull-apart pizza bread is ideal for serving with drinks and other snacks at a party. Dipping each dough ball in sauce before cooking allows you to get a beautifully crunchy, flavoursome crust on the edges and bottom of the bread. Switch up the flavours by swapping the pizza sauce for vegan pesto.*

**MAKES 12 ROLLS • PREPARATION TIME 30 MINUTES • COOKING TIME 1¾ HOURS**

# TEAR 'N' SHARE MARINARA BREAD

**FOR THE DOUGH**
450 g (14½ oz) strong white (bread) flour, plus extra for dusting
1 teaspoon sea salt
2 teaspoons sugar
7 g (about 2 teaspoons) fast-action dried yeast
1 tablespoon extra virgin olive oil
110 ml (3¾ fl oz) unsweetened almond milk
125 ml (4 fl oz) lukewarm water

**FOR THE MARINARA SAUCE**
200 ml (7 fl oz) passata (strained tomatoes)
1 tablespoon tomato purée
1 tablespoon olive oil
½ garlic clove, finely chopped or crushed
½ teaspoon dried oregano (optional)
20 g (¾ oz) Parmesan-style vegan cheese
salt and pepper

basil leaves, to garnish (optional)

Line the slow cooker pot with nonstick baking paper.

For the dough, put the dry ingredients into the bowl of a stand mixer fitted with a dough hook, add the oil and almond milk and mix briefly to combine. Gradually mix in the lukewarm water until you have a slightly sticky dough (you may not need all the water). Continue mixing on a low speed for 3–5 minutes until smooth and springy. Alternatively, mix the ingredients together with a wooden spoon in a large bowl, then turn the dough out on a lightly floured surface and knead by hand for 8–10 minutes until smooth and springy. Cover with clingfilm or a clean tea towel and leave to rest for 10–15 minutes.

Meanwhile, mix all the sauce ingredients together in a bowl. Season.

Divide the dough evenly into 12 pieces. Roll each into a ball and dip into the sauce. Allow the excess sauce to drip off and put the balls into the slow cooker to form an even layer. Reserve the remaining sauce. Cover with the lid and cook on low for 45 minutes until risen and puffy. Place a tea towel or kitchen paper underneath the slow cooker lid, re-cover the cooker and cook on high for 45 minutes.

Remove the tea towel or kitchen paper, top the rolls with a few tablespoons of the reserved sauce and grate over the cheese. Position the lid slightly ajar, then cook, still on high, for a further 15 minutes.

Lift the rolls out of the slow cooker using the lining paper and serve warm, garnished with basil leaves, if you like.

## FOR THE MOUSSAKA

3 tablespoons extra virgin
   olive oil
1 large butternut squash, peeled,
   deseeded and very thinly
   sliced
400 g (13 oz) meat-free mince
1 red onion, finely chopped
1 garlic clove, finely chopped
400 g (13 oz) can plum
   tomatoes
1 tablespoon vegan bouillon
   stock powder
1 teaspoon dried oregano
½ teaspoon dried mint
1 teaspoon ground cinnamon
1 tablespoon tomato purée
2 teaspoons Marmite
salt and pepper

## FOR THE BÉCHAMEL SAUCE

2 tablespoons vegetable oil
3 tablespoons cornflour
400 ml (14 fl oz) soya or
   unsweetened almond milk
1 bay leaf
½ teaspoon onion powder
¼ teaspoon freshly grated
   nutmeg
2 tablespoons nutritional yeast

green salad, to serve

*This hearty and satisfying Greek classic is given a slow-cooker makeover here, with squash providing a refreshing change from the traditional aubergine slices.*

**SERVES 4–6 • PREPARATION TIME 30–45 MINUTES
COOKING TIME 2–2½ HOURS**

# SQUASH MOUSSAKA

Grease the slow cooker pot with 1 tablespoon of the oil. Cover the bottom with a thin layer of squash slices, reserving the remainder.

Heat the remaining 2 tablespoons of oil in a large frying pan over a medium heat, add the meat-free mince and cook until golden brown. Add the onion and cook for 5 minutes until soft and translucent. Stir in the garlic and cook for a further minute. Add the tomatoes and break them up with a wooden spoon. Swill the tomato can out with water and pour in. Add the stock powder to the can, fill with boiling water, stir and pour in. Add the dried herbs, cinnamon, tomato purée, Marmite and plenty of seasoning and bring to the boil.

Spread a layer of this mixture over the squash. Repeat with 2 or 3 more alternating layers. Cover with the lid and cook on high for 1 hour.

Meanwhile, heat the vegetable oil in a small saucepan over a medium heat, add the cornflour and whisk for 1 minute until you have a smooth paste. Gradually add the dairy-free milk, whisking well after each addition. Add the remaining ingredients, bring to the boil, whisking constantly, and cook for about 10 minutes until thick and smooth. Remove the bay leaf, season and set aside. If your sauce is lumpy, blitz it in a blender or pass it through a sieve.

Spread the sauce evenly over the top of the moussaka, replace the lid, positioned slightly ajar, and cook, still on high, for another 1–1½ hours until the squash is easily pierced with a fork and the béchamel looks dry on top. Serve immediately with a simple green salad.

*This spicy katsu sauce is perfect teamed with ready-made breadcrumbed seitan or tofu fillets from the supermarket. The sauce freezes really well, so make a double batch and have it on hand for an emergency dinner party.*

**SERVES 6 • PREPARATION TIME 20 MINUTES • COOKING TIME 1 HOUR**

# KATSU CURRY SAUCE

2 carrots, peeled and finely
   chopped
2 onions, finely chopped
4 garlic cloves, finely chopped
20 g (¾ oz) fresh root ginger,
   peeled and finely grated
2 tablespoons plain flour
400 ml (14 fl oz) hot vegan
   bouillon stock
2 tablespoons garam masala
1 tablespoon curry powder
1 tablespoon maple syrup
1 tablespoon soy sauce
juice of 1 lime
1 teaspoon sea salt
1 bay leaf

TO SERVE
breadcrumbed seitan or tofu
fresh salad
sesame seeds
white rice
1 lime, cut into wedges

Put all the ingredients into the slow cooker, cover with the lid and cook on high for 1 hour, or on low for 3 hours.

Transfer the sauce mixture to a food processor and blitz until smooth. The sauce can be stored in an airtight container in the refrigerator for up to a week.

When ready to serve, heat the sauce up in a saucepan and serve over breadcrumbed seitan or tofu, along with some salad – thin matchsticks of carrot, cucumber, radish and chilli work really well – scattered with sesame seeds, rice and lime wedges.

*The majority of Sri Lankan cuisine is naturally vegan, and it makes the most of fresh produce by carefully considering each ingredient and pairing it with complementary spices. This recipe is perfect for that day in summer when you have a big bag of runner beans that you don't quite know what to do with. If you want to cook this at another time of year, when you can't get hold of runner beans, you can use fine green beans instead.*

**SERVES 4 • PREPARATION TIME 20 MINUTES • COOKING TIME 1½ HOURS**

# SRI LANKAN GREEN BEAN CURRY

2 tablespoons coconut oil, plus 1 tablespoon for the curry leaf garnish (optional)

2 tablespoons mustard seeds

10 fresh curry leaves, plus extra to garnish (optional)

1 tablespoon mild curry powder

1 teaspoon ground turmeric

¼ teaspoon ground cloves

1 large red onion, finely sliced

3 garlic cloves, finely sliced

500 g (1 lb) runner beans, trimmed, strings removed and cut on the diagonal into 2 cm (¾ inch) pieces

400 ml (14 fl oz) can coconut milk

2 large tomatoes, roughly chopped, or ½ x 400 g (13 oz) can chopped tomatoes

finely grated zest and juice of 1 unwaxed lime, plus extra lime wedges, to serve

salt (optional)

Heat the coconut oil in a small frying pan over a medium heat, add the mustard seeds and curry leaves and cook until the seeds begin to pop. Stir in the rest of the spices and cook for 1 minute.

Transfer the spice mixture to the slow cooker, add the onion, garlic and beans and toss to coat. Stir in the coconut milk and tomatoes. Fill the coconut tin with water and add to the slow cooker, then cover with the lid and cook on high for 1½ hours.

Season with the lime zest and juice, and salt if needed. If using curry leaves to garnish, fry in 1 tablespoon coconut oil until they have crisped up, then scatter over the finished dish. Serve immediately with lime wedges and rice or flatbreads.

*This cauliflower and potato curry is the ultimate comfort food and there couldn't be an easier slow cooker recipe than this one. Simply chuck all the ingredients in and sprinkle with herbs when it's done.*

**SERVES 4 • PREPARATION TIME 15 MINUTES • COOKING TIME 2¾ HOURS**

# ALOO GOBI

2 tablespoons vegetable oil
1 large cauliflower, broken
    into florets
300 g (10 oz) waxy potatoes,
    peeled and chopped into
    2–3 cm (¾–1¼ inch) chunks
1 onion, finely sliced
400 g (13 oz) can chopped
    tomatoes
15 g (½ oz) fresh root ginger,
    peeled and grated
2 garlic cloves, grated
2 teaspoons cumin seeds
½ teaspoon nigella seeds
1 tablespoon garam masala
1 teaspoon ground coriander
½ teaspoon ground turmeric
½ teaspoon chilli powder
juice of 1 lime
salt and pepper

small handful of coriander,
    roughly chopped, to garnish

Put all the ingredients, except the lime juice, into the slow cooker and season well with salt and pepper. Cover with the lid and cook on high for 2¾ hours, stirring once halfway through if you have the opportunity, until the potato and cauliflower are easily pierced with a fork.

Season with the lime juice and serve immediately, sprinkled with the chopped coriander, along with rice and/or flatbreads.

*The fiery, sweet and salty marinade used here for the cauliflower is very versatile, so feel free to use other vegetables of your choice. It works particularly well with small chunks of meaty aubergine, courgette and sweet potato – or try using tofu.*

**SERVES 4 • PREPARATION TIME 30 MINUTES • COOKING TIME 1 HOUR**

# CAULIFLOWER SATAY

**FOR THE SATAY SAUCE**
400 ml (14 fl oz) can coconut milk
finely grated zest and juice of 2 unwaxed limes, zest reserved to garnish
2 garlic cloves, finely chopped
2 tablespoons maple syrup
2 tablespoons soy sauce
150 g (5 oz) smooth peanut butter

**FOR THE CAULIFLOWER**
1 lemon grass stalk
1 shallot, peeled
2 garlic cloves, peeled
1 red chilli
20 g (¾ oz) fresh root ginger, peeled
1 tablespoon ground coriander
1 teaspoon ground cumin
½ teaspoon ground turmeric
3 tablespoons brown sugar
2 tablespoons dark soy sauce
1 cauliflower, broken into florets
2 tablespoons melted coconut oil
salt and pepper

Put all the satay sauce ingredients into the slow cooker, cover with the lid and cook on high for 1 hour.

Meanwhile, blitz together the lemon grass, shallot, garlic, chilli, ginger and ground spices in a food processor until you have a chunky paste. Transfer the spice mixture to a bowl, stir in the sugar and soy sauce and season to taste with salt and pepper. Add the cauliflower florets and toss until well coated in the mixture, then leave to marinate.

Preheat a griddle pan over a high heat. Remove the cauliflower florets from the marinade, toss in the coconut oil to coat and thread on to bamboo or wooden skewers (presoaked in water for 20 minutes to prevent burning), or metal skewers. Add to the hot pan and cook for 3–4 minutes on each side until caramelized and tender.

Serve garnished with the reserved lime zest, with the satay sauce for dipping.

*This curry is powerfully aromatic and a sure-fire crowd-pleaser, and will make your kitchen smell wonderfully inviting while it cooks. If you can't find Thai basil, substitute regular basil or use coriander instead. You can vary or increase the vegetable content, adding any thinly sliced stir-fry-appropriate vegetables or tossing in whole baby corn or mangetout at the same stage as the green beans and bamboo shoots.*

**SERVES 4 · PREPARATION TIME 15 MINUTES · COOKING TIME 2¾ HOURS**

# THAI GREEN CURRY

3 tablespoons Thai green
   curry paste
400 ml (14 fl oz) can
   coconut milk
2 aubergines, cut into wedges
1 red pepper, cored, deseeded
   and thinly sliced
2 tablespoons soy sauce
1 teaspoon sugar
1 red chilli, halved lengthways
   (optional)
6 kaffir lime leaves
200 g (7 oz) green beans,
   trimmed
225 g (7½ oz) can bamboo
   shoots, drained

TO SERVE
large handful of Thai basil leaves
large handful of coriander leaves
1 lime, cut into wedges
white rice

Fry the curry paste in a saucepan over a medium heat for about 1 minute until fragrant. Add half the coconut milk and stir until the paste has dissolved. Simmer for 3–4 minutes.

Transfer the curry paste mixture to the slow cooker and add the remaining coconut milk, the aubergines, the red pepper, soy sauce, sugar, chilli (if using) and lime leaves. Cover with the lid and cook on high for 2 hours until the aubergine is almost tender.

Stir in the green beans and bamboo shoots, replace the lid and cook, still on high, for a further 45 minutes.

Remove the red chilli and lime leaves. Serve immediately with the Thai basil, coriander, lime wedges and rice.

*This Middle Eastern-inspired dish is a total showstopper that you can have on the table after 3 hours of effortless cooking. If your cauliflower has fresh, perky leaves, try roasting them in the oven and using them to garnish – they have a deep flavour similar to roasted kale and it's a great way to prevent food waste. Simply toss the leaves with 1 tablespoon olive oil and season with salt and pepper, then spread out on a baking tray and roast in a preheated oven at 180°C (350°F), Gas Mark 4, for about 15 minutes.*

**SERVES 4 • PREPARATION TIME 15 MINUTES • COOKING TIME 1½–2 HOURS**

# WHOLE SPICED CAULIFLOWER

1 large cauliflower,
  leaves removed
2 tablespoons extra virgin
  olive oil
2 garlic cloves, grated
finely grated zest and juice of
  1 unwaxed lemon, plus extra
  zest and wedges to garnish
2 tablespoons tahini
1 tablespoon za'atar
1 tablespoon sesame seeds
1 teaspoon ground sumac
1 teaspoon ground cumin
½ teaspoon ground turmeric
salt and pepper

TO SERVE
fresh herbs, such as coriander
  and/or dill
pomegranate seeds
hummus

Cut a thin slice off the bottom of the cauliflower so that it will sit flat in the slow cooker pot.

Use 1 tablespoon of the oil to grease the slow cooker pot.

Put the remaining tablespoon of oil and all the other ingredients into the slow cooker and stir together well until you have a smooth paste. Dip the cauliflower into the paste, rubbing it all over, working it into all its nooks and crannies.

Sit the cauliflower in the slow cooker pot and season well with salt and pepper. Cover with the lid and cook on high for 1½–2 hours until the cauliflower is easily pieced with a fork.

Serve immediately, sprinkled with more salt, the lemon zest, fresh herbs and pomegranate seeds, along with hummus and lemon wedges.

*This cauliflower dish is inspired by the well-loved Sichuan kung pao stir-fry, which perfectly balances sweet, salty, spicy and sour flavours.*

**SERVES 4 • PREPARATION TIME 15 MINUTES • COOKING TIME 2½ HOURS**

# KUNG PAO CAULIFLOWER

1 large cauliflower, broken
   into florets
1 red pepper, cored, deseeded
   and thickly sliced
2 garlic cloves, grated
15 g (½ oz) fresh root ginger,
   peeled and grated
4 spring onions, thinly sliced,
   white and green parts kept
   separate
½ teaspoon chilli flakes
50 ml (2 fl oz) soy sauce
50 ml (2 fl oz) hot vegan
   bouillon stock
2 tablespoons hoisin sauce
2 tablespoons maple syrup
2 tablespoons rice vinegar
1 tablespoon sesame oil, plus
   extra for drizzling
1 tablespoon cornflour

TO SERVE
50 g (2 oz) roasted, salted
   peanuts, roughly chopped
small handful of coriander leaves
1 lime, cut into wedges

Put all the ingredients, except the cornflour, into the slow cooker and toss until well combined. Cover with the lid and cook on high for 2 hours.

Remove 2 tablespoons of the cooking liquid and mix with the cornflour in a cup until smooth. Stir the cornflour mixture into the cauliflower mixture, replace the lid and cook, still on high, for a further 30 minutes until the sauce has thickened.

Serve immediately, sprinkled with the chopped peanuts, coriander leaves and lime wedges.

*This aubergine mixture is the perfect balance of sweet and sour, with a deep umami richness – it's so moreish. Peeling the aubergines allows them to soak up more of the sauce and become really tender.*

**SERVES 4 • PREPARATION TIME 20 MINUTES • COOKING TIME 2 HOURS**

# MISO AUBERGINE NOODLES

2 large aubergines, peeled and cut into 2 cm (¾ inch) cubes

3 tablespoons sunflower or vegetable oil

200 g (7 oz) brown miso paste

75 ml (3 fl oz) rice vinegar

75 ml (3 fl oz) mirin

50 ml (2 fl oz) soy sauce

75 g (3 oz) sugar

TO SERVE

200 g (7 oz) dried buckwheat noodles

25 g (1 oz) walnuts, toasted and roughly chopped

2 tablespoons toasted sesame seeds

2 spring onions, finely sliced

1 lime, cut into wedges

Put the aubergines into the slow cooker with the oil and toss to coat.

Mix together the miso, vinegar, mirin, soy sauce and sugar in a small bowl. Pour the mixture over the aubergines, cover with the lid and cook on high for 2 hours, stirring occasionally, until meltingly tender. If the aubergines are not tender enough, replace the lid and cook, still on high, for 10-minute increments until ready.

When ready to serve, cook the noodles according to the packet instructions, then drain and toss with the aubergine mixture. Serve immediately, sprinkled with the walnuts, sesame seeds and spring onions, along with the lime wedges for squeezing over.

*This dish is inspired by a version I enjoyed at the prestigious Spanish restaurant Barrafina in London years ago. It's best to use Spanish paella rice here, as it holds its structure better than risotto rice. Weight measurements are given for the herbs in this instance, as their precise proportions are key to the flavour balance. This is lovely as a base for a charred cauliflower steak, with a sprinkle of paprika.*

**SERVES 4 • PREPARATION TIME 20 MINUTES • COOKING TIME 1½–2 HOURS**

# ARROZ VERDE

FOR THE RICE

2 tablespoons extra virgin olive oil

200 g (7 oz) paella rice

100 ml (3½ fl oz) dry white wine

250 ml (8 fl oz) hot vegan bouillon stock

FOR THE VERDE SAUCE

50 g (2 oz) pine nuts, toasted

20 g (¾ oz) spinach

20 g (¾ oz) flat leaf parsley, leaves and stalks

10 g (1/3 oz) basil, leaves and stalks

5 g (¼ oz) coriander, leaves and stalks

5 g (¼ oz) chervil, leaves and stalks (optional)

1 garlic clove, finely chopped or crushed

10 g (⅓ oz) sea salt flakes

50 ml (2 fl oz) extra virgin olive oil

250 ml (8 fl oz) water

Heat the oil for the rice in a large saucepan over a high heat. Add the rice and toss to coat, then cook, stirring regularly, for 3 minutes until lightly toasted. Add the white wine and allow it to bubble up and reduce until there is no liquid left visible in the pan.

Transfer the rice to the slow cooker and add the hot stock. Cover with the lid and cook on high for 2 hours, stirring once halfway through cooking, until the rice has absorbed almost all the liquid and is cooked but still firm to the bite. However, check for doneness after 1½ hours and thereafter at frequent intervals until ready. If it seems too dry, add a splash of water.

Meanwhile, blitz all the verde sauce ingredients in a food processor until smooth. Alternatively, finely chop the pine nuts, spinach and herbs, then use a pestle and mortar to pound them with the garlic and salt to a chunky paste. Gradually work in the oil, then mix in the measured water.

When the rice is done, stir through the verde sauce until well coated and serve immediately.

*Sweet potatoes cooked in the slow cooker are incredibly tender and buttery. Here they are served Mexican style with vegan chilli, but you could simply top them with some heated canned beans or cooked grains with peppers. You can also cook the sweet potatoes whole in the foil and then halve and top them later, adding 5–10 minutes to the cooking time.*

**SERVES 4 • PREPARATION TIME 15 MINUTES • COOKING TIME 2¾ HOURS**

# LOADED SWEET POTATOES

4 sweet potatoes, scrubbed and halved lengthways

2 tablespoons extra virgin olive oil

1 tablespoon ground cumin

400 g (13 oz) ready-made or homemade vegan chilli (see page 80)

1 red pepper, cored, deseeded and chopped

salt and pepper

TO SERVE

small bunch of coriander, finely chopped

1 avocado, cut into small cubes

3 spring onions, finely sliced

Score the cut surfaces of the sweet potatoes in a cross-cross pattern. Coat all over with the oil, cumin and salt and pepper.

Lay a large sheet of foil in the slow cooker pot. Sit the sweet potatoes on the foil, bring the sides of the foil together over the potatoes and fold over to seal tightly. Cover with the lid and cook on high for 2 hours.

Unwrap the foil and top each sweet potato half with a few tablespoons of the chilli and a sprinkle of chopped red pepper. Reseal the foil, replace the lid and cook, still on high, for a further 45 minutes.

Serve warm, topped with the coriander, avocado and spring onions.

*This baked vegetable recipe is very flexible, equally delicious made with potatoes, leeks, parsnips or celeriac. A mandolin is your friend here for uniform and speedy slicing.*

**SERVES 4–6 • PREPARATION TIME 20 MINUTES, PLUS SOAKING COOKING TIME 3 HOURS**

# BEETROOT & SWEET POTATO GRATIN

2 tablespoons extra virgin olive oil

50 g (2 oz) cashew nuts, soaked in cold water overnight or in boiling water for 1 hour, then drained

2 garlic cloves, grated

2 tablespoons nutritional yeast

1 tablespoon white wine vinegar

250 ml (8 fl oz) hot vegan bouillon stock

400 g (13 oz) large beetroots, peeled and thinly sliced

400 g (13 oz) sweet potatoes, peeled and thinly sliced

2 thyme sprigs, leaves picked

salt and pepper

Grease the slow cooker pot with 1 tablespoon of the oil.

Blend together the cashew nuts, garlic, nutritional yeast and vinegar in a blender until you have a smooth paste, adding a splash of water to loosen if necessary. Stir into the hot stock in a jug and set aside.

Arrange the vegetable slices in concentric circles in the slow cooker pot – you can either lay the slices flat or sit them upright, depending on the look you like.

Pour the stock mixture over, sprinkle with most of the thyme leaves and season to taste with salt and pepper. Place a tea towel or kitchen paper underneath the slow cooker lid, cover the cooker and cook on high for 2½ hours.

Remove the lid and tea towel or kitchen paper and cook uncovered, still on high, for a further 30 minutes.

Serve immediately, sprinkled with the remaining thyme leaves.

# MAINS:
# MORE THAN
# 3 HOURS

3 tablespoons olive oil

1 onion, finely chopped

1 celery stick, finely chopped

1 large carrot, finely chopped

1 garlic clove, finely chopped

25 g (1 oz) dried porcini
mushrooms, crumbled or
roughly chopped

150 ml (¼ pint) boiling water

300 g (10 oz) chestnut
mushrooms, finely chopped

50 g (2 oz) dried red lentils

50 g (2 oz) dried green lentils

400 g (13 oz) can chopped
tomatoes

1 tablespoon tomato purée

3 thyme sprigs, leaves picked

2 teaspoons Marmite

1 tablespoon balsamic vinegar,
or more to taste

300 ml (½ pint) hot vegan
bouillon stock

salt and pepper

TO SERVE

450 g (14½ oz) dried spaghetti

grated Parmesan-style vegan
cheese

fresh basil leaves

*This meat-free version of the famous Italian sauce is not only perfect for enjoying the traditional way with pasta, but makes a great alternative base for a vegan shepherd's pie (see page 93), or add a sprinkling of ground cinnamon and use it for a meatless moussaka (see page 49). The food processor can be your helpful assistant in this recipe, blitzing any vegetable that calls for being 'finely chopped' in the ingredients list to save on prep time.*

**SERVES 4–6 • PREPARATION TIME 25 MINUTES
COOKING TIME 7–8 HOURS**

# VEGAN BOLOGNESE

Heat the oil in a large frying pan over a medium-low heat, add the onion, celery and carrot with a pinch of salt and sauté for 5–10 minutes until beginning to soften and colour. Add the garlic and sauté for a further minute.

Meanwhile, put the porcini mushrooms into the slow cooker, pour over the measured boiling water and leave to soak.

Transfer the onion mixture to the slow cooker and add all the remaining ingredients, seasoning lightly with salt and pepper. Cover with the lid and cook on low for 7–8 hours. Check and adjust the seasoning, perhaps adding a dash more vinegar if needed.

When ready to serve, cook the spaghetti in a large saucepan of salted boiling water according to the packet instructions. Drain and toss with the sauce. Serve immediately, with some Parmesan-style vegan cheese grated over, garnished with a few basil leaves.

*This Brazilian stew freezes beautifully, so it's an ideal recipe to make in a big batch. Using the liquid that the canned beans come in helps to thicken the sauce and make it rich and creamy. It's great served with brown rice and plenty of freshly chopped herbs.*

**SERVES 4–6 • PREPARATION TIME 20 MINUTES • COOKING TIME 6–8 HOURS**

# BLACK BEAN STEW (FEIJOADA)

2 tablespoons olive oil

1 large onion, finely chopped

3 garlic cloves, finely chopped or crushed

small handful of coriander, leaves picked, chopped and reserved for garnishing, stalks finely chopped

2 x 400 g (13 oz) cans black beans (do not drain and rinse)

400 g (13 oz) can chopped tomatoes

2 sweet potatoes or carrots, peeled and cut into 2 cm (¾ inch) cubes

2 bay leaves

1 teaspoon smoked paprika

1 teaspoon ground coriander

1 teaspoon chipotle chilli powder

pinch of ground cloves

juice of 1 orange

salt and pepper

Heat the oil in a frying pan over a medium heat, add the onion and sauté for about 10 minutes until soft, translucent and beginning to colour. Add the garlic and coriander stalks and cook for a further minute.

Transfer the onion mixture to the slow cooker and add the black beans and their can liquid, tomatoes, sweet potatoes or carrots, bay leaves and spices. Season well with salt and pepper. Cover with the lid and cook on low for 6–8 hours until the sweet potato or carrot is easily pierced with a fork, and the smoky flavour is pronounced.

Season with the orange juice and serve immediately, sprinkled with the chopped reserved coriander leaves.

*The slow cooker makes this French vegetable stew completely fuss free. It's gorgeous served on its own or you could stir it through pasta as a chunky meatless ragu sauce.*

**SERVES 6–8 • PREPARATION TIME 20 MINUTES • COOKING TIME 6–8 HOURS**

# RATATOUILLE

2 large aubergines, halved
    lengthways and sliced into
    5 mm (¼ inch) half moons
2 red onions, halved lengthways
    and sliced into 5 mm (¼ inch)
    half moons
1 red pepper, cored, deseeded
    and chopped into 2 cm
    (¾ inch) cubes
1 yellow pepper, cored, deseeded
    and chopped into 2 cm
    (¾ inch) cubes
2 large courgettes, halved
    lengthways and sliced into
    5 mm (¼ inch) half moons
4 large tomatoes, cut into
    8 wedges
2 garlic cloves, grated
2 tablespoons tomato purée
1 tablespoon balsamic vinegar,
    or more to taste
1 tablespoon sugar, or more
    to taste
salt and pepper

large handful of basil leaves,
    to serve

Put all the ingredients into the slow cooker and toss until well combined. Season well with salt and pepper. Cover with the lid and cook on low for 6–8 hours until all the vegetables are tender and have created their own thick, jammy sauce.

Check and adjust the seasoning, adding more sugar or balsamic vinegar if needed. Serve immediately, sprinkled with the basil leaves.

*This caponata is highly customizable. Swap the black olives for green, throw some butternut squash or sweet potato in to bulk it out more and use whatever vinegar you have sitting around – balsamic and red wine vinegar, for instance, work just as well. The key here is to achieve a powerful agrodolce flavour – a balance of sweet and sour.*

**SERVES 4 • PREPARATION TIME 30 MINUTES • COOKING TIME 7 HOURS**

# SLOW-COOKED CAPONATA

4 tablespoons extra virgin
  olive oil
2 large aubergines, cut into 2 cm
  (¾ inch) cubes
2 celery sticks, finely sliced
2 red onions, finely sliced
4 garlic cloves, finely sliced
400 g (13 oz) can plum
  tomatoes
3 tablespoons sherry vinegar
1 tablespoon light brown soft
  sugar
50 g (2 oz) black olives
50 g (2 oz) raisins
3 tablespoons capers in brine,
  drained
salt and pepper

**TO SERVE**
large handful of basil leaves
toasted pine nuts

Heat 3 tablespoons of the oil in a large frying pan over a medium-high heat, add the aubergines and sauté for 3–5 minutes until beginning to soften and colour. Transfer to the slow cooker.

Heat the remaining tablespoon of oil in the frying pan, add the celery and onions and sauté for 5–8 minutes until translucent and lightly golden brown. Stir in the garlic and cook for a further minute.

Transfer the celery and onion mixture to the slow cooker and add the tomatoes, squeezing them between your hands to break them up, vinegar and sugar. Season well with salt and pepper. Cover with the lid and cook on low for 6 hours until all the vegetables are very tender.

Stir in the olives, raisins and capers, replace the lid and cook, still on low, for a further hour until well reduced.

Check and adjust the seasoning, then serve immediately, sprinkled with the fresh basil leaves and toasted pine nuts.

*This makes a big vat of soup and freezes beautifully, so it's great as a batch-cook recipe. It's perfect for when there is a surplus of tomatoes in the summer – use ones that are really ripe and maybe even getting a bit wrinkly. As an alternative option, transfer the finished soup to a saucepan and simmer briskly on the hob, without the lid, until it has thickened and reduced, then serve as a simple pasta sauce with spaghetti.*

**SERVES 8 • PREPARATION TIME 20 MINUTES • COOKING TIME 6–8 HOURS**

# CLASSIC TOMATO SOUP

2 tablespoons olive oil, plus extra
    for drizzling
1 kg (2 lb) tomatoes, roughly
    chopped
1 carrot, finely chopped
1 red pepper, cored, deseeded
    and finely chopped
3 garlic cloves, halved
1 tablespoon sugar (optional)
500 ml (17 fl oz) hot vegan
    bouillon stock
2 bay leaves
2 thyme sprigs
2 basil sprigs, plus extra leaves to
    garnish
salt and pepper

croutons, to serve (optional)

Put the oil, tomatoes, carrot, red pepper, garlic, sugar, if using, and hot stock into the slow cooker. Add the bay leaves and herb sprigs and season well with salt and pepper. Cover with the lid and cook on low for 6–8 hours until the vegetables are very tender and the soup mixture smells strongly aromatic. (You can cook the soup on high for 3 hours if you want to enjoy it sooner.)

Use an immersion blender to blend the soup mixture until smooth and creamy, or leave it to cool and blitz in a food processor. Alternatively, mash with a potato masher to a chunky purée.

Reheat the soup if necessary and serve immediately, garnished with basil leaves and black pepper, drizzled with olive oil and sprinkled with croutons, if you like.

*Polenta made in the conventional way is such a labour-intensive dish that we often end up passing on it, but it comes out perfectly from the slow cooker with so little effort. If you're making it in advance, you may need to stir through a splash more stock or almond milk to loosen when reheating to serve, as it sets when it cools. Spread any leftovers in a thin layer in a deep baking tray, leave to cool and firm, and then slice into bars about 3.5 cm (1½ inches) wide for deep-frying in oil until golden brown, like chips.*

**SERVES 4 • PREPARATION TIME 5 MINUTES • COOKING TIME 6½ HOURS**

# CREAMY POLENTA

175 g (6 oz) polenta
800 ml (1¼ pints) hot vegan bouillon stock
2 tablespoons nutritional yeast
150 ml (¼ pint) unsweetened almond milk
salt and pepper

Put the polenta, hot stock and nutritional yeast into the slow cooker and mix together well. Cover with the lid and cook on low for 6 hours until the polenta is creamy and soft.

Whisk in the almond milk until well combined, replace the lid and cook, still on low, for a further 30 minutes.

Season to taste with salt and pepper and serve immediately, topped with jackfruit burger mixture (see page 99), Bolognese sauce (see page 70) or spicy bean chilli (see page 80).

*This spicy Moroccan stew couldn't be easier to bring together and yet has buckets of flavour. To make it go further, try adding a couple of 400 g (13 oz) cans of chickpeas, drained, for the last hour of cooking.*

**SERVES 4 • PREPARATION TIME 20 MINUTES • COOKING TIME 6–8 HOURS**

# HARISSA RED LENTIL & SQUASH STEW

2 tablespoons extra virgin
   olive oil

1 large onion, finely sliced

4 garlic cloves, finely sliced

1 large butternut squash, peeled,
   deseeded and cut into 2 cm
   (¾ inch) cubes

200 g (7 oz) dried red lentils

1 tablespoon harissa paste,
   or more to taste

2 teaspoons ground cumin

1 teaspoon ground cinnamon

1 teaspoon ground turmeric

400 g (13 oz) can chopped
   tomatoes

300 ml (½ pint) hot vegan
   bouillon stock

finely grated zest and juice of
   1 unwaxed lemon

salt and pepper

large handful of coriander, finely
   chopped, to serve

Heat the oil in a large frying pan over a medium heat, add the onion and sauté for about 10 minutes until soft and translucent. Add the garlic and cook for a further minute.

Transfer the onion mixture to the slow cooker and add the butternut squash, lentils, harissa paste, spices, tomatoes and hot stock. Season well with salt and pepper. Cover with the lid and cook on low for 6–8 hours until the squash and lentils are tender and the sauce has thickened.

Season to taste with more harissa and the lemon zest and juice, then serve immediately, sprinkled with the freshly chopped coriander.

*This mixed bean chilli is perfect for warming up a long, cold winter's evening. It's very forgiving, so if you forget about it in the slow cooker for a few hours, there is no need to worry.*

**SERVES 8 • PREPARATION TIME 30 MINUTES • COOKING TIME 6 HOURS**

# SPICY BEAN CHILLI

3 tablespoons extra virgin olive oil

400 g (13 oz) chestnut mushrooms, finely chopped

2 onions, finely chopped

1 celery stick, finely chopped

3 garlic cloves, grated

2 teaspooons ground cumin

2 teaspoons ground coriander

1 teaspoon smoked paprika

1 teaspoon dried oregano

1–2 teaspoons hot chilli powder

2 tablespoons plain flour

1 teaspoon sugar

3 tablespoons tomato purée

2 teaspoons soy sauce

450 ml (¾ pint) hot vegan bouillon stock

400 g (13 oz) can chopped tomatoes

400 g (13 oz) can red kidney beans, drained and rinsed

400 g (13 oz) can mixed beans, drained and rinsed

salt and pepper

TO SERVE

handful of coriander, finely chopped

1 lime, cut into wedges

rice or bread (optional)

Heat 2 tablespoons of the oil in a large frying pan over a medium heat, add the mushrooms and cook until all the moisture they release has evaporated and they are beginning to turn golden brown. Transfer to the slow cooker.

Add the remaining oil to the frying pan and sauté the onions and celery for about 6 minutes until soft and translucent. Stir in the garlic and cook for a further minute, followed by the spices, cooking for 2 minutes. Add the flour and cook, stirring, for 2 more minutes.

Transfer the onion mixture to the slow cooker and add the sugar, tomato purée, soy sauce, hot stock and tomatoes. Cover with the lid and cook on low for 5 hours.

Stir in the beans, replace the lid and cook, still on low, for 1 hour.

Season well with salt and pepper and serve immediately, sprinkled with finely chopped coriander and with lime wedges for squeezing over, along with rice or bread, if you like.

*This is a great hands-free way to make the most of these two under-appreciated vegetables, which are deeply earthy, sweet and nutty in flavour. A perfect winter warmer with a fiery chilli kick. As an alternative, you could blitz the cooked mixture in a food processor into a warming soup.*

**SERVES 4 • PREPARATION TIME 20 MINUTES • COOKING TIME 4 HOURS**

# BRAISED CELERIAC & SWEDE

1 celeriac
1 swede, peeled and cut into
    1 cm (½ inch) cubes
2 tablespoons olive oil
1 fennel bulb, finely sliced
1 onion, finely sliced
1 red chilli, deseeded and finely
    chopped
2 thyme sprigs
200 ml (7 fl oz) hot vegan
    bouillon stock
finely grated zest and juice of
    1 unwaxed lemon

handful of flat leaf parsley, finely
    chopped, to serve

Prepare the celeriac by using a serrated knife to trim off the top and bottom, then use the knife to peel the celeriac (a vegetable peeler isn't robust enough) and cut into rough 1 cm (½ inch) cubes.

Put the celeriac, swede, oil, fennel, onion, chilli, thyme and hot stock into the slow cooker, cover with the lid and cook on low for 4 hours until the celeriac and swede are easily pierced with a fork.

Stir through the lemon zest and juice and serve immediately, sprinkled with finely chopped parsley.

*A deeply flavoursome broth is so easily achievable with a slow cooker, as with this Vietnamese-style pho, to which you can add noodles, seasonal vegetables, fresh herbs and condiments of your choice. Some fried chunks of firm tofu can also be added to make a more substantial dish.*

**MAKES 2 LITRES (3½ PINTS) BROTH • PREPARATION TIME 20 MINUTES COOKING TIME 4–6 HOURS**

# AROMATIC PHO

1 onion, halved
1 whole piece of fresh root ginger, peeled and halved lengthways
1 carrot, peeled and halved lengthways
3 garlic cloves, peeled and bashed
1 celery stick, halved lengthways
8 dried shiitake mushrooms
1 teaspoon sugar
1 teaspoon salt
2 star anise
1 lemon grass stalk, bashed
1 cinnamon stick
1 teaspoon black peppercorns
1 teaspoon coriander seeds
1 teaspoon fennel seeds
2 tablespoons soy sauce
2 litres (3½ pints) cold water

TO SERVE
noodles
marinated tofu
fresh vegetables
Sriracha hot sauce
handful of coriander

Heat a frying pan over a high heat until searing hot. Add the onion and ginger halves cut side down and cook until charred.

Transfer the charred onion and ginger to the slow cooker and add all the remaining ingredients. Cover with the lid and cook on low for 4–6 hours.

Strain through a fine sieve or muslin and serve hot with dried pho noodles or other noodles of your choice, cooked separately according to the packet instructions, tofu and vegetables such as pak choi (quartered and either charred before adding or poached for a few minutes in the broth), sliced spring onions and red chillies. Sriracha hot sauce and fresh coriander sprigs will provide extra punches of flavour.

*This sweet and ever so slightly sour stew is rich and hearty. You could leave out whichever toppings you want to serve with it for your guests to help themselves.*

**SERVES 4 • PREPARATION TIME 25 MINUTES • COOKING TIME 8 HOURS**

# PERSIAN AUBERGINE STEW

3 tablespoons olive oil

1 onion, finely chopped

3–4 garlic cloves, finely chopped

2 teaspoons ground cinnamon

1 tablespoon cardamom pods, crushed, seeds removed and ground

2 teaspoons cumin seeds, ground

1 teaspoon ground turmeric

2 aubergines, cut into 2 x 4 cm (¾ x 1½ inch) wedges

2 x 400 g (13 oz) cans chopped tomatoes

1 tablespoon pomegranate molasses

1 tablespoon sugar

salt and pepper

TO SERVE

ready-made crispy shallots

handful of fresh herbs, such as parsley, mint, dill and/or coriander, chopped

pomegranate seeds

flatbreads, warmed

Heat the oil in a frying pan over a medium heat, add the onion and sauté for about 8–10 minutes until soft and translucent. Stir in the garlic and spices and cook for 1 minute.

Transfer the onion mixture to the slow cooker and add all the remaining main ingredients. Cover with the lid and cook on low for 8 hours, checking occasionally and adding a splash of water if the stew looks dry.

Season the stew to taste with salt and pepper and serve, sprinkled with the ready-made crispy shallots, fresh herbs and pomegranate seeds, with warmed flatbreads on the side. Some toasted flaked almonds scattered over make a tasty addition too.

*This curry packs a powerful punch of flavour. Swap the tofu for cauliflower or any other vegetable if you're not a tofu fan, but I guarantee you'll be mopping up every last bit of this rich sauce.*

**SERVES 6–8 • PREPARATION TIME 20 MINUTES, PLUS PRESSING COOKING TIME 7–9 HOURS**

# TOFU TIKKA MASALA

2 x 400 g (13 oz) cans chopped tomatoes

2 tablespoons coconut oil

4 garlic cloves, finely chopped or grated

20 g (¾ oz) fresh root ginger, peeled and finely grated

6–8 cardamom pods (use black cardamom if available, otherwise green is fine)

2 cinnamon sticks

1 tablespoon garam masala

1 teaspoon ground cumin

½ teaspoon chilli powder

½ teaspoon ground turmeric

500 g (1 lb) silken tofu, drained and cut into 2.5 cm (1 inch) cubes

1 teaspoon dried fenugreek leaves (methi), crumbled

2 tablespoons sugar

200 ml (7 fl oz) coconut cream

salt and pepper

TO SERVE

small handful of coriander

1 lemon, cut into wedges

rice

Blitz the tomatoes in a food processor until smooth. Transfer to the slow cooker.

Heat the coconut oil in a frying pan over a medium heat, and the garlic and ginger and sauté for about 3 minutes until fragrant and golden. Stir in the cardamom pods, cinnamon sticks and ground spices and cook for a further minute.

Transfer the spice mixture to the slow cooker, cover with the lid and cook on low for 6–8 hours.

Stir in the tofu cubes, fenugreek leaves, sugar and coconut cream, replace the lid and cook on high for 1 hour.

Season to taste with salt and pepper and serve immediately, sprinkled with the coriander leaves and with lemon wedges for squeezing over, along with rice on the side.

*A soup for healthy days, and great for clearing out the vegetable drawer of the refrigerator. Use whatever greens you have on hand – green beans, cabbage and Brussel sprouts are all good additions.*

**SERVES 4 • PREPARATION TIME 20 MINUTES • COOKING TIME 6¼ HOURS**

# ALL THE GREENS SOUP

2 tablespoons coconut oil
1 shallot, finely sliced
4 garlic cloves, grated
20 g (¾ oz) fresh root ginger, peeled and grated
2 celery sticks, finely sliced
1 large head of broccoli, broken into florets and stalks roughly chopped
2 courgettes, roughly chopped
500 ml (17 fl oz) hot vegan bouillon stock
1 teaspoon ground turmeric
1 teaspoon ground coriander
400 g (13 oz) kale or spinach, any tough stalks removed
finely grated zest and juice of 1 unwaxed lime
1 tablespoon soy sauce

**TO GARNISH**
coconut cream
large handful of coriander leaves
black and white sesame seeds

Heat the coconut oil in a frying pan over a medium heat, add the shallot, garlic and ginger and sauté for 3 minutes until fragrant.

Transfer to the slow cooker and add the celery, broccoli, courgettes, hot stock, turmeric and ground coriander. Cover with the lid and cook on low for 6 hours. (You can cook the soup on high for 2–3 hours if you want to enjoy it sooner.)

If using kale, stir in, replace the lid and cook, still on low, for a further 15 minutes until wilted and tender. If using spinach, simply stir through for about 5 minutes until just wilted.

Use an immersion blender to blitz the soup until smooth, adding some water if you prefer a thinner consistency. Season to taste with the lime zest, lime juice and soy sauce.

Serve immediately, garnished with a swirl of coconut cream and the coriander leaves, sprinkled with black and white sesame seeds.

*This vibrant orange soup, full of warming Eastern flavours, is incredibly easy to put together. When making soups in your slow cooker, a handy formula to keep in mind is to use 800 g–1 kg (1 ¾–2 lb) of prepared vegetables to 800 ml (1¼ pints) of liquid for a balanced result.*

**SERVES 4–6 • PREPARATION TIME 25 MINUTES • COOKING TIME 6 HOURS**

# CURRIED BUTTERNUT SQUASH SOUP

1 large butternut squash, peeled, deseeded and roughly chopped (about 800 g–1 kg/1¼–2 lb prepared weight)

1 onion, roughly chopped

3 garlic cloves, roughly chopped

20 g (¾ oz) fresh root ginger, peeled and roughly chopped

400 ml (14 fl oz) can coconut milk

400 ml (14 fl oz) hot vegan bouillon stock

1 tablespoon garam masala

½ teaspoon ground coriander

½ teaspoon ground cumin

½ teaspoon chilli powder

½ teaspoon ground ginger

salt and pepper

TO GARNISH (OPTIONAL)

small handful of coriander, roughly chopped

1 red chilli, finely sliced

1 tablespoon coconut flakes, toasted

Put all the main ingredients into the slow cooker, cover with the lid and cook on low for 6 hours until the squash is extremely tender.

Use an immersion blender to blend the soup until smooth, adding a splash of water if it seems too thick.

Serve hot, sprinkled with the coriander, chilli and toasted coconut flakes, if you like.

*This earthy dahl has a Thai-style kick to it – warming, sweet but with a spicy sharp edge – which makes a welcome change. If you have leftover parsnips from a roast, sprinkle them with cumin, warm through in the oven and serve on top of the dahl for a texture contrast.*

**SERVES 6 • PREPARATION TIME 20 MINUTES • COOKING TIME 6–8 HOURS**

# GREEN PARSNIP DAHL

2 tablespoons coconut oil

2 shallots, finely chopped

20 g (¾ oz) fresh root ginger, peeled and finely grated

4 garlic cloves, finely chopped or crushed

60 g (2¼ oz) Thai green curry paste

1 teaspoon ground turmeric

400 g (13 oz) can green lentils, drained and rinsed

400 ml (14 fl oz) can coconut milk

3 large parsnips, peeled and finely chopped

750 ml (1¼ pints) hot vegan bouillon stock

300 g (10 oz) leafy greens, such as kale, chard or spinach, any tough stalks removed

1 tablespoon soy sauce

2 tablespoons lime juice

large handful of coriander, finely chopped

Heat the coconut oil in a large saucepan over a medium heat, add the shallots, ginger and garlic and sauté for 8 minutes until the shallots are soft and translucent and everything smells fragrant. Stir in the curry paste and turmeric and cook for a further minute.

Transfer the curry paste mixture to the slow cooker and add the lentils, coconut milk, parsnips and hot stock. Season with salt and pepper. Cover with the lid and cook on low for 6–8 hours until the lentils are tender and creamy, stirring once or twice during cooking if you have the opportunity.

Stir in the kale or chard, if using, 15 minutes before the end of the dahl cooking time, replacing the lid and cooking, still on low, until wilted and tender. If using spinach, simply stir through for about 5 minutes until just wilted.

Season with the soy sauce and lime juice and stir through the coriander. Serve immediately with rice or on its own with some dairy-free yogurt.

2 tablespoons melted coconut oil

2 large onions, peeled

4 garlic cloves, peeled

25 g (1 oz) fresh root ginger, peeled

2 green chillies

large handful of coriander, leaves picked and reserved for garnishing, stalks finely chopped

small handful of fresh curry leaves

2 tablespoons ground cumin

1 tablespoon ground coriander

1 tablespoon black mustard seeds

1½ teaspoons ground turmeric

1 teaspoon ground cinnamon

3 tablespoons tomato purée

400 g (13 oz) dried split red lentils, rinsed

400 ml (14 fl oz) can coconut milk

750 ml (1¼ pints) hot vegan bouillon stock

8 carrots, peeled and grated

300 g (10 oz) leafy greens, such as kale, chard or spinach, any tough stalks removed

salt and pepper

FOR THE ROASTED CARROTS (OPTIONAL)

3 carrots, peeled and cut into wedges

2 tablespoons melted coconut oil

1 teaspoon ground cumin

1 tablespoon maple syrup

TO SERVE

pickled red onions

1 lime, cut into wedges

*This recipe makes great use of a grater so that everything comes together easily and super speedily. It's delicious on its own or with rice and poppadums.*

**SERVES 6 • PREPARATION TIME 25 MINUTES COOKING TIME 6–8 HOURS**

# CARROT DAHL

Heat the coconut oil in a large saucepan over a medium heat and grate the onions, garlic, ginger and green chillies straight into the pan. Add the coriander stalks and cook for 10 minutes until the onion is soft and translucent and everything smells fragrant. Stir in the curry leaves, spices and tomato purée and cook for a further minute.

Transfer the onion and spice mixture to the slow cooker and add all the remaining main ingredients, except the greens. Season with salt and pepper. Cover with the lid and cook on low for 6–8 hours until the lentils are tender and creamy, stirring once or twice during cooking if you have the opportunity.

About an hour before you are ready to eat, if making the roasted carrots, preheat the oven to 200°C (400°F), Gas Mark 6. Toss the carrot wedges with the coconut oil and cumin, spread out on a baking tray and roast in the oven for 30–35 minutes, drizzling with the maple syrup 10 minutes before the end of the roasting time, until tender and caramelized at the edges.

If using kale or chard, stir into the carrot dahl 15 minutes before the end of the dahl cooking time, replacing the lid and cooking, still on low, until wilted and tender. If using spinach, simply stir through for about 5 minutes until just wilted.

Serve the dahl immediately, topped with the roasted carrots, if using, and sprinkled with the reserved coriander leaves, along with pickled red onions and the lime wedges for squeezing over.

## FOR THE FILLING

1 large onion, finely chopped

2 celery sticks, finely chopped

2 carrots, peeled and finely chopped

2 garlic cloves, grated

2 thyme sprigs, leaves picked

2 rosemary sprigs, leaves picked and finely chopped

300 g (10 oz) dried Puy or beluga (black) lentils, rinsed

400 g (13 oz) can chopped tomatoes

2 tablespoons red wine vinegar

1 tablespoon sugar

250 ml (8 fl oz) hot vegan bouillon stock

250 g (8 oz) frozen peas

## FOR THE TOPPING

3 sweet potatoes, peeled and roughly chopped

3 tablespoons extra virgin olive oil

finely grated zest and juice of 1 unwaxed lemon

¼ teaspoon freshly grated nutmeg

salt and pepper

*Topping this hearty stew with sweet and creamy potatoes spiked with zesty lemon makes it a year-round supper staple rather than only for the winter. If you've already got some vegan Bolognese sauce (see page 70) in the freezer after a big-batch cook, you could defrost and use in place of the filling here, simply stirring through the frozen peas. Then top with the sweet potato mash and cook as instructed below.*

**SERVES 4 • PREPARATION TIME 30 MINUTES COOKING TIME 7–9 HOURS**

# SHEPHERD'S PIE

Put all the ingredients for the filling, except the frozen peas, into the slow cooker, cover with the lid and cook on low for 6–8 hours until the vegetables are tender and the lentils are cooked through.

Meanwhile, cook the sweet potatoes for the topping in a large saucepan of salted boiling water for about 10 minutes until easily pierced with a fork. Drain in a colander and leave to steam for 2 minutes. Mash the sweet potato with a potato masher or fork in a bowl and mix through the oil, lemon zest and juice, nutmeg and plenty of salt and pepper. Cover with clingfilm and set aside until the filling is done.

Stir the frozen peas into the cooked filling and season well with salt and pepper, then top with the sweet potato mash. Place a tea towel or kitchen paper underneath the slow cooker lid, cover the cooker and cook on high for 1 hour. Alternatively, transfer the filling and peas to an ovenproof dish, top with the sweet potato mash and cook under a preheated medium grill for 20 minutes until well browned. Serve immediately.

*This pie filling is so intensely creamy and rich that you will hardly believe that it's dairy free. Most shop-bought pastry is now vegan, which makes this speedy dinner a breeze. The filling also works well as a creamy stew, so serve with rice or potatoes for a change or if you want to skip the extra step of cooking the pastry.*

**SERVES 4–6 • PREPARATION TIME 1 HOUR, PLUS SOAKING COOKING TIME 4–5 HOURS**

# MUSHROOM, LEEK & THYME PIE

2 tablespoons sunflower or vegetable oil

2 large leeks, trimmed, cleaned and sliced

500 g (1 lb) button mushrooms, halved

4 garlic cloves, finely chopped

2 thyme sprigs, leaves picked, plus extra leaves to garnish

200 g (7 oz) cashew nuts, soaked in cold water overnight or in boiling water for 1 hour, then drained

500 ml (17 fl oz) hot vegan bouillon stock

2 tablespoons nutritional yeast

1 teaspoon miso paste

finely grated zest and juice of 1 unwaxed lemon

1 sheet of vegan puff pastry

1 tablespoon dairy-free milk, to glaze

salt and pepper

Heat the oil in a large frying pan over a medium heat, add the leeks and mushrooms and sauté for 10 minutes until the leeks are softened and the mushrooms are beginning to colour. Stir in the garlic and thyme leaves and cook for a further minute. Transfer to the slow cooker.

Blitz the cashew nuts, hot stock, nutritional yeast, miso paste and lemon zest and juice in a food processor or blender until smooth and creamy. Pour over the leek and mushroom mixture and stir to combine. Season with pepper, and salt if needed. Cover with the lid and cook on low for 4–5 hours until the sauce has thickened and the mushrooms are very soft. Add a splash of water or dairy free milk if the mixture seems too stiff.

Preheat the oven to 190°C (375°F), Gas Mark 5. If your slow cooker pot is ovenproof, remove it from the cooker, top with the sheet of puff pastry, trim the excess around the edge and crimp to secure. Use a pastry brush to brush the pastry with the dairy-free milk to glaze and bake in the oven for 30–40 minutes until the pastry is golden brown. Alternatively, transfer the filling to an ovenproof dish, then top with the pastry, glaze and bake in the same way.

Serve immediately, sprinkled with the extra thyme leaves.

*Potatoes cooked in their skins in the slow cooker take on a deeper, more nutty flavour than their regular oven-baked counterparts. They are so quick to prepare before you set out to work and will be all ready for when you get home.*

**SERVES 4 • PREPARATION TIME 10 MINUTES • COOKING TIME 8 HOURS**

# SLOW-COOKED JACKET POTATOES

4 large baking potatoes,
    scrubbed
1 tablespoon olive oil
1 tablespoon sea salt flakes

Prick the potatoes all over with a fork and rub with the olive oil and sea salt.

Wrap each potato individually in foil. Put the wrapped potatoes into the slow cooker, cover with the lid and cook on low for 8 hours until easily pierced with a fork.

Split open and serve immediately with a topping of your choice, such as canned or homemade baked beans (see page 25), vegan chilli (see page 80), Bolognese sauce (see page 70), ratatouille (see page 73), meatless meatballs (see page 39) or jackfruit burger mixture (see page 99).

nonstick cooking spray or vegan
butter, for greasing
1 parsnip, peeled and cut into
large chunks
1 carrot, peeled and cut into
large chunks
2 tablespoons olive oil
1 red onion, finely chopped
2 garlic cloves, finely chopped
1 rosemary sprig, leaves picked
and finely chopped
2 thyme sprigs, leaves picked
2 sage sprigs, leaves picked and
finely chopped
2 tablespoons chopped flat leaf
parsley, plus extra to garnish
½ teaspoon ground allspice
½ teaspoon ground nutmeg
180 g (6 oz) cooked chestnuts,
roughly chopped
200 g (7 oz) mushrooms, finely
chopped
300 g (10 oz) mixed nuts,
toasted and roughly chopped
100 ml (3½ fl oz) hot vegan
bouillon stock
100 g (3½ oz) fresh
breadcrumbs
100 g (3½ oz) dried cranberries
salt and pepper

pomegranate seeds, to garnish

*This nut roast is so good, it will have the meat eaters around the table trying to get a look in. It also keeps really well in an airtight container or covered in foil in the refrigerator for up to 3 days.*

**SERVES 6–8 • PREPARATION TIME 1 HOUR
COOKING TIME 4 HOURS**

# FESTIVE NUT ROAST

Line the bottom and sides of a silicone or metal 900 g (2 lb) loaf tin with nonstick baking paper and grease with cooking spray or vegan butter. Ensure that the tin fits snugly (use some balls of foil to secure it if it doesn't quite reach the cooker bottom). Pour in enough water to come 2 cm (¾ inch) up the sides of the pot.

Cook the parsnip and carrot in a large saucepan of salted boiling water for about 10 minutes. Drain and leave to steam for 5 minutes. Transfer to a bowl and mash with a fork.

Heat the oil in a large frying pan over a medium heat, sauté the onion for 8–10 minutes until translucent. Add the garlic and cook for a further minute. Stir in the herbs and spices and cook for 2 minutes until fragrant. Add the chestnuts, mushrooms and nuts and cook for 5–8 minutes until the mushrooms have released all their moisture and the pan looks a little dry. Stir in the remaining ingredients and cook for 2–3 minutes until the stock has been absorbed.

Take the pan off the heat, stir through the parsnip and carrot and season to taste. Transfer the mixture to the prepared loaf tin, using the back of a spatula or spoon to push it down and make sure it is evenly spread. Place a tea towel or kitchen paper underneath the slow cooker lid, cover the cooker and cook on high for 4 hours until the nut roast is firm to the touch and no wet patches are visible.

Turn out of the tin and serve immediately, sprinkled with plenty of extra chopped parsley and pomegranate seeds.

*These meaty and moreish burgers bring a real taste of barbecue indoors with minimal effort. You can also use the burger mixture to top jacket potatoes (see page 96) or polenta (see page 78).*

**SERVES 4 • PREPARATION TIME 25 MINUTES • COOKING TIME 6 HOURS**

# PULLED JACKFRUIT BURGERS

2 tablespoons sunflower or
    vegetable oil
1 onion, finely sliced
400 g (13 oz) can young jackfruit,
    drained and rinsed
300 ml (½ pint) vegan cider
150 ml (¼ pint) tomato ketchup
50 ml (2 fl oz) soy sauce
50 ml (2 fl oz) apple cider vinegar
50 g (2 oz) dark brown soft sugar
1 teaspoon ground ginger
½ teaspoon cayenne pepper
1 teaspoon smoked paprika
½ teaspoon freshly grated nutmeg
2 teaspoons garlic powder
salt and pepper

FOR THE SLAW
200 g (7 oz) mixed red and white
    cabbage, shredded
1 carrot, peeled and cut into fine
    matchsticks
2 spring onions, finely sliced
finely grated zest and juice of
    1 unwaxed lime
2 tablespoons sunflower oil

4 burger buns, halved and toasted,
    to serve

Heat the oil in a frying pan over a medium heat, add the onion and sauté for about 8 minutes until softened and lightly golden. Add the jackfruit and cook for a further 5 minutes.

Transfer the jackfruit mixture to the slow cooker and add the remaining main ingredients, seasoning well with salt and pepper. Cover with the lid and cook on low for 6 hours until the jackfruit pulls apart easily with 2 forks.

Mix together the cabbage, carrot and spring onions for the slaw in a bowl. Whisk together the lime zest and juice and oil, pour over the vegetables and toss to coat.

Shred the jackfruit mixtutre and serve immediately in toasted burger buns, topped with the slaw.

*A stuffed pepper can feel a bit dated, but they're incredibly delicious and so simple to knock together that they deserve a spot back on our dinner tables. If peppers aren't your thing, try stuffing scooped-out large beef tomatoes or hollowed-out courgette halves instead. Or stuff half a butternut squash, deseeded with a little of the flesh removed to leave a substantial border, and cook for an extra 30–45 minutes until tender.*

**SERVES 4–6 • PREPARATION TIME 20 MINUTES • COOKING TIME 6 HOURS**

# MEXICAN STUFFED PEPPERS

4–6 large peppers, any colour
   or a mixture
125 g (4 oz) quinoa
200 g (7 oz) can black beans,
   drained and rinsed
200 g (7 oz) can sweetcorn
   kernels, drained and rinsed,
   or frozen and defrosted
200 g (7 oz) passata (strained
   tomatoes)
1 garlic clove, grated
1 tablespoon chipotle paste
2 teaspoons ground cumin
1 teaspoon sweet smoked paprika
salt and pepper

TO SERVE
small handful of coriander
sliced avocado
1 lime, cut into wedges

Slice the stalks and tops off the peppers and discard. Use a teaspoon or small serrated knife to remove the cores and seeds, taking care not to cut through the pepper flesh. Add 2 cm (¾ inch) of water to the slow cooker pot and arrange the peppers upright in the pot so that they fit snugly together.

Mix all the remaining ingredients together in a large bowl and season with salt and pepper. Spoon the filling evenly into the pepper shells, cover with the lid and cook on low for 6 hours until the quinoa is cooked through and the pepper shells have softened.

Serve immediately sprinkled with coriander leaves, along with avocado slices and lime wedges for squeezing over.

# SWEET TREATS

*To make this a real showstopper, alternate slices of blood orange with the bread slices. This looks particularly stunning and the rind cooks down until it is soft and delicious. This pudding feels like an incredibly indulgent breakfast for dessert.*

**SERVES 6 • PREPARATION TIME 15 MINUTES • COOKING TIME 2–2½ HOURS**

# ZESTY MARMALADE BREAD & BUTTER PUDDING

50 g (2 oz) vegan butter, plus extra for greasing
6 thick slices of stale bread, sliced diagonally in half into triangles
3 tablespoons marmalade
1 unwaxed orange, thinly sliced
170 g (6 oz) silken tofu
250 ml (8 fl oz) dairy-free milk
115 g (4 oz) light brown soft sugar
1 teaspoon vanilla bean paste
finely grated zest of 1 unwaxed orange

TO SERVE
icing sugar
dairy-free custard

Grease the slow cooker pot with vegan butter. Spread each triangle of bread with the vegan butter, on both sides, and spread the marmalade on one side of each. Arrange the bread slices in the slow cooker pot, cut edge down, so that they fit snugly together and look like mountain peaks. Nestle a slice of orange into each gap.

Blitz the tofu, dairy-free milk, brown sugar and vanilla bean paste in a food processor until smooth. Pour over the bread slices and sprinkle the orange zest on top.

Place a tea towel or kitchen paper underneath the slow cooker lid, cover the cooker and cook on high for 2–2½ hours until the bread has absorbed most of the liquid and the top is beginning to look a little golden.

Remove the slow cooker pot from the cooker, uncover and leave to cool slightly and firm up, then serve warm, dusted with icing sugar, along with dairy-free custard.

*Incredibly nostalgic and easy, a slow cooker gives this classic pudding a moist and airy texture. You can also make individual sponges using 5 or 6 mini pudding tins or dariole moulds, following the same method but reducing the cooking time by an hour.*

**SERVES 6–8 • PREPARATION TIME 25 MINUTES, PLUS STANDING**
**COOKING TIME 3–4 HOURS**

# SYRUP SPONGE

85 g (3 oz) vegan butter, plus extra for greasing
75 g (3 oz) golden syrup
140 ml (4¾ fl oz) soya milk
½ tablespoon apple cider vinegar
85 g (3 oz) caster sugar
1 teaspoon vanilla bean paste
175 g (6 oz) self-raising flour
1 teaspoon baking powder
½ teaspoon salt
finely grated zest of 1 unwaxed lemon

dairy-free custard, to serve

Grease a 1 litre (1¾ pint) pudding basin liberally with vegan butter, pour in the golden syrup and set aside.

Mix together the soya milk and vinegar in a small bowl and leave to curdle for about 10 minutes.

Put the vegan butter, sugar and vanilla bean paste into the bowl of a stand mixer fitted with the whisk attachment, and whisk together until pale and fluffy, or whisk with a hand whisk in a bowl.

Mix together the remaining ingredients in a separate bowl. Fold into the sugar and butter mixture half at a time, alternating with the curdled soya milk half at a time, until all the ingredients are combined and no dry patches remain and you have a smooth batter.

Pour the batter into the pudding basin. Top a sheet of foil with one of greased nonstick baking paper, fold together in a narrow pleat down the centre and place, greased side down, over the basin. Secure around the basin rim with a long length of string. Pass the string over the top of the basin and tie to the other side to create a handle. Put the pudding basin into the slow cooker. Pour in enough boiling water to come halfway up the sides. Cover with the lid and cook on high for 3–4 hours until a skewer inserted into the centre comes out clean.

Use the handle to lift the pudding basin out of the cooker, peel back the foil and paper and leave to stand for 5 minutes before turning out on to a plate to serve, with some dairy-free custard on the side.

*Ginger and rhubarb were made to be together – fiery meets sweet and tart. Having said that, this crisp and crunchy crumble topping sits well on any seasonal fruit. If you can't find stem ginger, just add a teaspoon of ground ginger to the filling.*

**SERVES 4–6 • PREPARATION TIME 20 MINUTES • COOKING TIME 4 HOURS**

# RHUBARB, APPLE & GINGER CRUMBLE

FOR THE CRUMBLE TOPPING
200 g (7 oz) plain flour
90 g (3¼ oz) demerara sugar
50 g (2 oz) rolled oats
1 teaspoon ground ginger
pinch of salt
160 g (5½ oz) vegan butter, chilled and cut into small cubes

FOR THE FILLING
600 g (1¼ lb) Bramley apples, peeled, cored and cut into 2.5 cm (1 inch) chunks
300 g (10 oz) rhubarb, cut into 4 cm (1½ inch) chunks
250 g (8 oz) caster sugar
15 g (½ oz) fresh root ginger, peeled and grated
1 tablespoon chopped stem ginger in syrup
½ tablespoon cornflour
finely grated zest and juice of 1 unwaxed lemon

Mix together all the dry ingredients for the crumble topping in a bowl. Add the butter and rub in with your fingertips until the mixture resembles fine breadcrumbs. Set aside.

Put all the filling ingredients into the slow cooker and toss until well combined. Top with the crumble mixture. Lay 2 sheets of kitchen paper directly on top of the crumble. Cover with the lid and cook on low for 3½ hours until the fruit is tender.

Remove the kitchen paper, position the lid slightly ajar and cook, still on low, for a further 30 minutes until the crumble topping is crisp.

*The sponge is so light and airy and the sauce so deeply flavoured that this is sure to become a staple of your slow cooker repertoire. Make double the sauce, as it freezes well for emergency situations!*

**MAKES 5–6 PUDDINGS • PREPARATION TIME 25 MINUTES, PLUS SOAKING & COOLING COOKING TIME 1–1½ HOURS**

# STICKY TOFFEE PUDDING

FOR THE CARAMEL SAUCE
50 g (2 oz) vegan butter, plus extra for greasing
1 tablespoon cornflour
250 ml (8 fl oz) almond milk
125 g (4 oz) light brown soft sugar
1 tablespoon black treacle
1 teaspoon sea salt flakes

FOR THE PUDDING
150 g (5 oz) pitted dates, finely chopped
1 teaspoon bicarbonate of soda
75 ml (3 fl oz) coconut oil, melted
190 ml (6½ fl oz) almond milk
1 teaspoon vanilla bean paste
75 ml (3 fl oz) maple syrup
3 tablespoons date syrup
300 g (10 oz) plain flour
3 teaspoons baking powder

dairy-free custard, to serve

Grease 5 or 6 (check how many fit in your slower cooker pot) mini pudding tins or dariole moulds with vegan butter.

Put the cornflour and 3 tablespoons of the almond milk into a saucepan over a gentle heat and whisk into a smooth, thick paste. Turn the heat up to medium and cook, whisking, for 1 minute. Gradually add the remaining almond milk, whisking constantly. Add the butter, sugar and treacle and bring to the boil, whisking, then leave to boil for 5–8 minutes, whisking occasionally, until slightly thickened (it will set further when cooled). Whisk in the sea salt. Place 2 tablespoons of the sauce into the bottom of each tin or mould and leave to cool, reserving the remaining sauce.

Meanwhile, just cover the dates and bicarbonate of soda with water in a small bowl and leave to soak for 15–30 minutes until soft.

Whisk together the coconut oil, almond milk, vanilla bean paste, soaked dates with their liquid and the syrups in a large bowl until well combined. Sift in the flour and baking powder, then fold in gently until smooth and no dry patches remain. Carefully pour the batter into the tins or moulds until they are three-quarters full (you may have some leftover), then put them in the slow cooker. Cover with the lid and cook on high for 1–1½ hours until the puddings are firm.

Remove and leave to cool and firm up for 5 minutes, then carefully turn them out. Serve with the sauce and dairy-free custard.

*Creamy, smooth and moreish, this rice pudding has such a silky finish thanks to the rich coconut milk.*

**SERVES 6 • PREPARATION TIME 5 MINUTES • COOKING TIME 2–2½ HOURS**

# COCONUT RICE PUDDING

nonstick cooking spray or vegan butter, for greasing
100 g (3½ oz) pudding rice
400 ml (14 fl oz) can coconut milk
400 ml (14 fl oz) unsweetened almond milk or soya milk
125 g (4 oz) light brown soft sugar
1 cinnamon stick

a dollop of jam, to serve

Grease the slow cooker pot with nonstick cooking spray or vegan butter.

Put all the ingredients into the slow cooker, cover with the lid and cook on high for 2–2½ hours until the rice is very tender and the mixture has thickened but is still creamy.

Discard the cinnamon stick and serve immediately with a dollop of jam for an old-school pudding. Alternatively, keep things tropical by sprinkling with dessicated coconut or coconut shavings and roughly chopped pistachio nuts, and serving with chopped mango, pineapple or banana.

*An elegant dessert that is perfect for a fuss-free dinner party. I like to halve the pears so that they stay submerged in the liquid, but you could keep them whole and turn halfway through cooking. A pinch of saffron threads would add a lovely rich colour to the pears.*

**SERVES 6 • PREPARATION TIME 20 MINUTES • COOKING TIME 3–4 HOURS**

# POACHED CARDAMOM PEARS

500 ml (17 fl oz) pear juice
150 g (5 oz) golden caster sugar
rind and juice of 1 unwaxed
   lemon
20 g (¾ oz) fresh root ginger,
   peeled and thinly sliced
15 g (½ oz) fresh root turmeric,
   peeled and thinly sliced, or
   ½ teaspoon ground turmeric
10 cardamom pods, lightly
   bashed
1 cinnamon stick
pinch of salt
6 pears, peeled and halved
   lengthways, stalks left intact

Put the pear juice and sugar into a saucepan and heat gently until the sugar has dissolved, then bring to the boil.

Transfer the hot syrup to the slow cooker and add the lemon rind and juice, ginger, turmeric, cardamom pods, cinnamon stick and salt. Nestle the pears into the slow cooker. Cover with the lid and cook on low for 3–4 hours, or on high for 1–2 hours, until the pears are tender but not mushy, the timing depending on the size and firmness of the pears.

Serve the pears warm or cold with some of the syrup.

*Any leftovers of this incredibly rich chocolate cake will keep well in the refrigerator, covered in foil, for up to 3 days. The sauce is absorbed into the cake slightly so it ends up tasting like a fudgy brownie – you could reheat it in the microwave before serving.*

**SERVES 6–8 • PREPARATION TIME 20 MINUTES, PLUS COOLING
COOKING TIME 3–4 HOURS**

# CHOCOLATE LAVA SLAB

nonstick cooking spray or vegan butter, for greasing
125 g (4 oz) plain flour
150 g (5 oz) caster sugar
3 tablespoons cocoa powder
2 teaspoons baking powder
½ teaspoon salt
125 ml (4 fl oz) dairy-free milk
75 ml (3 fl oz) sunflower or vegetable oil
1 teaspoon vanilla bean paste
150 g (5 oz) vegan dark chocolate chips (optional)

FOR THE TOPPING
150 g (5 oz) light brown soft sugar
3 tablespoons cocoa powder
350 ml (12 fl oz) freshly brewed hot coffee, or 1 tablespoon instant coffee powder mixed with 350 ml (12 fl oz) boiling water

Grease the slow cooker pot with vegan butter and line the bottom and sides with nonstick baking paper, or simply grease with nonstick cooking spray.

Mix together the dry ingredients in a large bowl until well combined. Add the dairy-free milk, oil and vanilla bean paste and whisk until combined, but take care not to overmix. Fold in the chocolate chips, if using, or reserve them for sprinkling over the batter.

Pour the batter into the slow cooker and spread it out evenly, then sprinkle over the chocolate chips, if using and not already added.

Mix together the brown sugar and cocoa powder in a jug, add the hot coffee and whisk to combine. Pour the hot sauce carefully over the cake batter (you can pour it over the back of a dessert spoon to make sure the flow of water doesn't disturb your batter) and leave it to sit on top, without stirring in. Cover with the lid and cook on low for 3–4 hours or until a skewer inserted into the top half of the cake comes out clean (don't be misled by the saucy layer on the bottom).

Remove the slow cooker pot from the cooker, uncover and leave the cake to cool and firm up for at least 15 minutes before serving.

*These rolls take the fuss out of baking. You don't need to wait for the dough to rise, as the slow cooker does the job, so just put them in at night and wake up to gorgeous freshly cooked buns in the morning.*

**MAKES 8–10 ROLLS • PREPARATION TIME 25 MINUTES, PLUS RESTING COOKING TIME 1½–2 HOURS**

# CINNAMON TAHINI ROLLS

### FOR THE ROLLS
50 g (2 oz) vegan butter
2 tablespoons caster sugar
250 ml (8 fl oz) almond milk
7 g (about 2 teaspoons) fast-action dried yeast
400 g (13 oz) plain flour, plus extra for dusting
1 teaspoon sea salt

### FOR THE FILLING
75 g (3 oz) vegan butter
3 teaspoons ground cinnamon
1 teaspoon ground mixed spice
5 tablespoons light brown soft sugar
2 tablespoons tahini

### FOR THE ICING
50 g (2 oz) icing sugar
3 tablespoons tahini
1–2 tablespoons almond milk

Melt the butter, sugar and almond milk and leave to cool. Stir in the yeast and leave to stand for about 5 minutes until it starts to foam.

Put the flour and salt into the bowl of a stand mixer fitted with a dough hook, add the yeast mixture and mix until a dough forms. Continue mixing on a low speed for 3–5 minutes until smooth and springy. Alternatively, mix the ingredients together with a wooden spoon in a large bowl, then turn out onto a lightly floured surface and knead by hand for 8–10 minutes until smooth and springy. Cover with a clean tea towel and leave to rest for 10–15 minutes.

Meanwhile, mix together all the filling ingredients in a bowl.

Sprinkle the dough with a little flour and roll out on a lightly floured surface to about 30 x 40 cm (12 x 16 inches). Spread the filling over, right to the edges. Starting from a longer edge, roll the dough into a cylinder. Use a floured serrated knife to cut into 5 cm (2 inch) slices.

Line the bottom of the slow cooker with nonstick baking paper so that it comes at least 2 cm (¾ inch) up the sides. Place the rolls on their sides in the pot, spaced evenly apart. Place a tea towel or kitchen paper underneath the lid, cover and cook on high for 2 hours until the inner rolls are firm to the touch (check for doneness after 1½ hours and thereafter at frequent intervals until cooked).

Mix the icing ingredients to a spreadable consistency, adding more milk if necessary. Spread over the rolls while warm and serve immediately.

*These toffee-coloured peanut butter blondies are halfway between a brownie and a cookie. The edges turn wonderfully crisp and chewy, while the centre is fudgy and soft.*

**MAKES 12 BARS • PREPARATION TIME 20 MINUTES, PLUS COOLING COOKING TIME 1½–2 HOURS**

# PEANUT BUTTER BLONDIE COOKIE BARS

2 tablespoons ground flaxseed (linseed)

4 tablespoons cold water

nonstick cooking spray or vegan butter, for greasing

200 g (7 oz) light brown soft sugar

80 g (3 oz) vegan butter

250 g (8 oz) peanut butter

1 teaspoon vanilla extract

150 g (5 oz) plain flour

¼ teaspoon baking powder

125 g (4 oz) vegan dark chocolate chips or 70% cocoa vegan dark chocolate, chopped

Mix the ground flaxseed with the measured cold water in a small bowl and leave to stand for about 5 minutes until thickened.

Meanwhile, line the bottom of the slow cooker pot with nonstick baking paper and grease the sides with vegan butter or nonstick cooking spray.

Put the sugar, vegan butter, peanut butter and vanilla extract into the bowl of a stand mixer fitted with the whisk attachment and whisk together until well combined, or whisk with a hand whisk in a bowl. Add the flaxseed mixture and mix until smooth. Fold in the flour and baking powder until no dry patches remain, then fold in half the chocolate chips.

Pour the batter into the slow cooker and spread it out evenly, then sprinkle over the remaining chocolate chips. Cover with the lid, positioned slightly ajar, and cook on high for 1½–2 hours until golden around the edges and a skewer inserted into the centre comes out clean.

Uncover and leave to cool in the slow cooker pot for at least an hour until firmer and easier to remove. Then turn out and cut into 12 bars.

*If you're not a fan of blueberries, this recipe makes a showstopping lemon drizzle cake without them. Any citrus works well for the drizzle, so try making it with orange or lime. If you have a citrus zester, use it to make long curls of zest for an elegant finishing touch.*

**MAKES ONE 900 G (2 LB) LOAF CAKE • PREPARATION TIME 20 MINUTES, PLUS STANDING & COOLING • COOKING TIME 2 HOURS**

# LEMON BLUEBERRY DRIZZLE

**FOR THE CAKE**
nonstick cooking spray or vegan butter, for greasing
250 ml (8 fl oz) unsweetened soya milk
1 teaspoon apple cider vinegar
75 ml (3 fl oz) sunflower or vegetable oil
1 teaspoon vanilla bean paste
350 g (11½ oz) plain flour
2 teaspoons baking powder
1½ teaspoons bicarbonate of soda
½ teaspoon salt
150 g (5 oz) light brown soft sugar
2 tablespoons finely grated unwaxed lemon zest
2 tablespoons lemon juice
250 g (8 oz) blueberries

**FOR THE DRIZZLE ICING**
100 g (3½ oz) icing sugar
finely grated zest and juice of 1 unwaxed lemon

Line the bottom and sides of a silicone or metal 900 g (2 lb) loaf tin with nonstick baking paper and grease with cooking spray or vegan butter. Ensure that the tin fits snugly inside the slow cooker (use some balls of foil to secure it if it doesn't quite reach the cooker bottom).

Mix together the almond milk and vinegar in a bowl and leave to curdle for about 10 minutes. Then add the oil and vanilla bean paste and whisk together until well combined.

Mix together all the remaining cake ingredients, except the blueberries, in a large separate bowl. Gradually fold in the almond milk mixture and blueberries until well combined.

Pour the batter into the prepared loaf tin and spread it evenly. Place a tea towel or kitchen paper underneath the lid, cover the cooker and cook on high for 2 hours until risen and firm to the touch, and a skewer inserted into the centre comes out clean.

Remove from the slow cooker and leave to cool in the tin for 10 minutes. Then use the lining paper to lift the cake out of the tin and leave it to cool completely on a wire rack.

Put the icing sugar into a small bowl and use a small whisk or spoon to mix the lemon juice in gradually until you have a fairly thick icing, adding 1–2 teaspoons of water to loosen if necessary. Spread over the cake and sprinkle with the lemon zest.

*A retro classic that never loses its appeal. It's best to use canned pineapple here, as fresh has a a bit too much juice. You have to be pretty fearless to turn this cake out, but with a little faith it does work, although to save yourself the worry you could use a slow cooker liner.*

**SERVES 4–6 • PREPARATION TIME 20 MINUTES, PLUS COOLING
COOKING TIME 2½–3 HOURS**

# PINEAPPLE UPSIDE DOWN CAKE

nonstick cooking spray or vegan butter, for greasing
50 g (2 oz) vegan butter, melted
100 g (3½ oz) light brown soft sugar
8–10 pineapple rings from a can, drained, with 50 ml (2 fl oz) of the syrup reserved
about 10 glacé cherries (1 per pineapple slice), without stalks
225 g (7½ oz) plain flour
200 g (7 oz) caster sugar
1 teaspoon bicarbonate of soda
½ teaspoon salt
120 ml (4 fl oz) unsweetened almond milk
80 ml (3 fl oz) sunflower or vegetable oil
1 teaspoon vanilla bean paste
1 tablespoon white wine vinegar

vegan ice cream or dairy-free custard, to serve

Grease the slow cooker pot with nonstick cooking spray or vegan butter.

Put the melted vegan butter into the slow cooker and sprinkle evenly with the brown sugar. Arrange the pineapple rings to cover the bottom of the pot, cutting and trimming off any excess to allow them to come right to the sides as necessary. Place a cherry in the centre of each ring.

Sift the dry ingredients into a large bowl and mix to combine. Add all the remaining ingredients, including the reserved pineapple syrup, and whisk together until you have a smooth batter.

Pour the batter over the pineapple slices and spread it out evenly. Cover with the lid and cook on high for 2½–3 hours until a skewer inserted into the centre comes out clean.

Remove the slow cooker pot from the cooker, uncover and leave the cake to cool for at least 15 minutes. Upturn a serving plate over the top of the pot and carefully flip the plate and pot together to turn the cake out on to the plate. If your slow cooker is quite deep, find a dish that fits snugly inside so that you can put your hand directly on the bottom of the dish when flipping, or cut a piece of cardboard or a cake board to size.

Serve warm or cold with vegan ice cream or dairy-free custard.

*This cake is so soft and moist, and will keep in an airtight container for up to a week – perfect for unexpected visitors at teatime.*

**MAKES ONE 900 G (2 LB) LOAF CAKE • PREPARATION TIME 20 MINUTES, PLUS COOLING COOKING TIME 2–2½ HOURS**

# GINGER CAKE

nonstick cooking spray or vegan
   butter, for greasing
2 tablespoons ground flaxseed
   (linseed)
4 tablespoons cold water
200 g (7 oz) plain flour
2 teaspoons bicarbonate of soda
1 tablespoon ground ginger
1 teaspoon ground mixed spice
   or allspice
½ teaspoon salt
85 g (3 oz) vegan butter
85 g (3 oz) black treacle
85 g (3 oz) golden syrup
85 g (3 oz) dark brown soft sugar
140 ml (4¾ fl oz) almond milk
25–50 g (1–2 oz) stem ginger in
   syrup, to taste, finely chopped

Line the bottom and sides of a silicone or metal 900 g (2 lb) loaf tin with nonstick baking paper and grease with nonstick cooking spray or vegan butter. Ensure that the tin fits snugly inside the slow cooker pot, using some scrunched-up balls of foil to raise the tin slightly off the bottom, or to secure it if it doesn't quite reach the cooker bottom.

Mix the ground flaxseed with the measured cold water in a small bowl and leave to stand for about 5 minutes until thickened.

Meanwhile, sift the flour, bicarbonate of soda, spices and salt into a bowl and set aside.

Heat the vegan butter, black treacle, golden syrup and sugar in a saucepan over a gentle heat until just melted, then remove from the heat and beat into the flour mixture. Add the flaxseed mixture and the almond milk and mix until smooth. Fold in the stem ginger.

Pour the batter into the prepared tin. Place a tea towel or kitchen paper underneath the lid, cover the cooker and cook on high for 2–2½ hours until a skewer inserted into the centre comes out clean.

Remove from the slow cooker and leave to cool in the tin for 10 minutes. Then use the lining paper to lift the cake out of the tin and leave to cool completely on a wire rack before serving.

*This delicious apple butter is such a versatile sweet topping to keep on hand. For a speedy pudding, spread it on a puff pastry base and top with sliced apples or berries.*

**MAKES ONE 500 G (1 LB) JAR • PREPARATION TIME 15 MINUTES, PLUS COOLING COOKING TIME 8–10 HOURS**

# APPLE BUTTER

8–10 apples, peeled, cored and
    roughly chopped
8–10 pitted dates, roughly
    chopped
50 g (2 oz) light brown soft
    sugar
1 tablespoon ground cinnamon
½ teaspoon freshly grated
    nutmeg
1 tablespoon vanilla extract
½ teaspoon sea salt flakes

ice cream, toast or yogurt and
    granola, to serve

Put all the ingredients into the slow cooker, cover with the lid and cook on low for 8–10 hours, stirring occasionally, until the mixture has thickened and looks dark brown and jammy.

Remove the slow cooker pot from the cooker, uncover and leave to cool in the pot. Then use an immersion blender to blend the apple mixture until smooth.

Spoon the apple butter into a sterilized jar, seal and store in the refrigerator for up to 2 weeks. Serve warm with ice cream, spread on toast or on top of yogurt and granola, or enjoy on its own with an extra sprinkling of ground cinnamon.

*This deep, rich sauce doesn't retain any of the coconut flavour of the milk by the time it's fully caramelized, so it's a great neutral-tasting caramel to suit any dessert.*

**MAKES ONE 400 G (14 OZ) JAR • PREPARATION TIME 5 MINUTES
COOKING TIME 5–6 HOURS**

# SALTED CARAMEL SAUCE

400 ml (14 fl oz) can coconut
   milk
250 g (8 oz) light brown soft
   sugar
1 teaspoon vanilla bean paste
1–2 teaspoons sea salt flakes,
   to taste

vegan ice cream

Put the coconut milk, sugar and vanilla bean paste into the slow cooker. Cover with the lid and cook on low for 2 hours. Position the lid slightly ajar and cook, still on low, for a further 3–4 hours, stirring occasionally, until the sauce turns from pale to deep brown, smells sweet and rich, and has reduced in volume. Depending on the brand of coconut milk, you may find that by the end of cooking the sauce is a little lumpy. If so, pass through a sieve or blend in a food processor until smooth.

Stir through the sea salt. Transfer to a sterilized jar, seal and store in the refrigerator for up to 2 weeks.

Serve over vegan ice cream. Or you could dollop it on top of coconut rice pudding (see page 111) or use as an alternative sauce for sticky toffee pudding (see page 110).

# INDEX